POLITICAL LIFE IN THE
·CITY OF ROME

Current and forthcoming titles in the Classical World Series

Classical World Series

POLITICAL LIFE IN THE CITY OF ROME

John R. Patterson

Bristol Classical Press

General Editor: John H. Betts
Series Editor: Michael Gunningham

For Angela

Cover illustration:
A *denarius* of 63 BC, showing a Roman placing his
voting-tablet into the ballot box.
[Drawing by Vince Hewitt]

First published in 2000 by
Bristol Classical Press
an imprint of
Gerald Duckworth & Co. Ltd
61 Frith Street
London W1D 3JL
e-mail: inquiries@duckworth-publishers.co.uk
Website: www.ducknet.co.uk

Reprinted 2001

© 2000 by John R. Patterson

A catalogue record for this book is available
from the British Library

ISBN 1-85399-514-2

Printed in Great Britain by
Antony Rowe Ltd, Eastbourne

Contents

List of Illustrations

Preface

'Political life in the city of Rome' is a vast topic and in many respects a controversial one. What follows is simply an attempt to sketch out some central themes and issues. The selective bibliography is structured to parallel the main text, so the reader can pursue particular areas of interest further. The Latin terms for political institutions are often used in the text but I have endeavoured to explain them when they occur, and there is a glossary at the end of the volume.

I would like to offer my particular thanks to Michael Crawford, Peter Garnsey, Anna Mason, Henrik Mouritsen and Oliver Mulvey, who very helpfully read and commented on drafts of the book; they do not necessarily agree with the views expressed here, and errors which remain are my own responsibility. Sally Cann, Paolo Carafa, and Andrew Wallace-Hadrill kindly allowed me to use adapted versions of their drawings (Figs. 5 and 9, Fig. 4, and Fig. 1 respectively); the Soprintendenza Archeologica di Roma, and the Sovraintendenza Archeologica del Comune di Roma gave permission for the reproduction of photographs (Figs. 3 and 8, and Figs. 6 and 7 respectively). Thanks are also due to Jean Scott of Bristol Classical Press, to Nigel Cassidy and Aidan Foster for help with the illustrations, and to my editor Michael Gunningham for careful scrutiny which substantially improved the final text. My greatest debt is to Angela Heap, to whom the book is gratefully dedicated.

J.R.P.

Chapter 1
Introduction

The two elements in the title of this volume reflect the two central themes – 'political life' and 'the city of Rome' – which it seeks to interrelate. The volume deals primarily with the crucial period between the Roman victory at Zama in 202 BC following the Carthaginian invasion of Italy led by Hannibal, which resulted in Rome taking a leading role in the Mediterranean, and the outbreak of civil war in 49 BC, which led to the dictatorship of Julius Caesar, the collapse of the republican system of government in the Roman state, and the principate of Augustus. It is not, however, a narrative history of those years; and it does not discuss in detail the careers of famous or notorious political figures such as the Gracchus brothers, Marius, Sulla, Crassus and Pompey, who took a leading role in politics at that period (though their activities inevitably play a part from time to time). Instead, the book has a rather more restricted aim: to study the structures of Roman politics (as opposed to the careers of distinguished individuals); and to relate the patterns of Roman political life to the history and archaeology of the city of Rome itself.

Traditionally the study of the later Republic has been approached primarily through the literary sources which have survived from antiquity. This volume, however, also places a particular emphasis on the historical topography of the city of Rome, which has been revealed by detailed investigation over many years. Serious study of Rome's topography can be traced back to the Renaissance and beyond, but particular phases of interest took place in the 1810s (related to Napoleon's brief occupation of the city); the latter part of the nineteenth century (when the population of Rome, recently chosen as capital of a newly united Italy, grew substantially in size); the 1930s (when Mussolini's Fascist government was keen to emphasise its self-image as heir of the Roman Empire of antiquity); and most recently in the 1980s, when a major programme of restoration and study of Rome's monuments was put into effect. As a result of this programme of work, and a more general awareness of the importance of image-creation in the projection of political power, the study of the topography of the ancient city has in recent years become a central element in studies of Roman history, perhaps most strikingly in those dealing with the principate of Augustus (see, for example, the volume in this series on *Augustan Rome* by A. Wallace-Hadrill). A central theme of this book is that an awareness of the monuments of Rome is just as important in writing the history of the Roman Republic

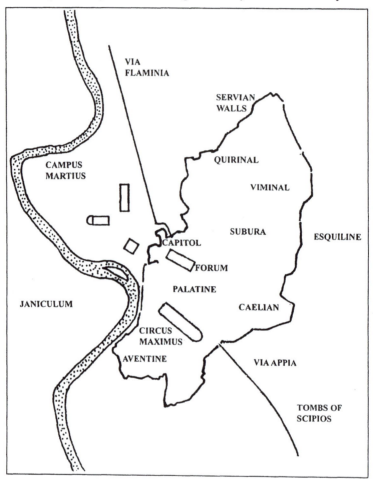

Fig 1 The City of Rome.

as that of the Empire, and especially so when politics is the focus of the enquiry. Virtually all buildings of the period, whether private houses, tomb-monuments, temples, porticoes or basilicas, had political implications of one kind or another, as indeed did more or less all the activities of the social and political elite of Rome. The construction of buildings was recorded in literary texts and their images appeared on coins, issued by ambitious politicians. The second and first centuries BC represent a period of lavish building and architectural experimentation in the city of Rome, as Romans spent the wealth they had obtained from the conquest of the lands round the Mediterranean – in the form of booty and taxes – on embellishing their city. In the process they adopted new architectural styles, often derived from Rome's increasingly close contact with the Greek world, and innovative building techniques. Thus the buildings of Rome were both the product of political competition and the backdrop for the day-to-day political activity which was played out in the Forum Romanum and other political meeting-places in the centre of the city. Orators addressing the Roman people exploited to the full the historical and symbolic associations of the buildings that surrounded the Forum.

The aim of this book, then, is to examine the nature of Roman politics in the last hundred and fifty years of the Republic, with a particular focus on its impact on the city. Chapter 2 briefly outlines the sources of information available to the historian, and discusses some of the problems involved in reconstructing the topography of the city of Rome. Chapter 3 explains in general terms the nature of the Roman political system, in particular the role of popular assemblies, senate and magistrates – setting them in their physical context in the city – and introduces some of the lively historical debates which have been generated in recent years as attempts have been made to match the practice of politics with theoretical views of the Roman constitution. Chapter 4 examines the phenomenon of aristocratic competition and investigates the ways in which the activities of the political elite at Rome – a strongly competitive group – left their mark on the city. Chapter 5 deals with the practicalities of politics – in particular canvassing, bribery and violence. A brief concluding chapter looks forward to the early Empire, examining the impact of a sole ruler – the emperor – on political life in the city, and discusses whether the advent of the principate brought about the end of politics.

One important point needs to be made clearly at the outset. The term 'politician', which I use occasionally to refer to the protagonists in political life, is a useful but misleading one. Although loose and fluctuating political alliances were central to the everyday business of politics, those participating in political activity did so not as members of a party held together by a common programme or ideology, but as individuals. That individualism (and its effects) is a central theme of the book.

Chapter 2
Problems of interpretation

The literary sources

Our knowledge of the political system of the mid and late Republic rests very largely on the wealth of literary sources available for these periods. Interpreting these texts and using them to reconstruct how politics worked in practice is, however, for a variety of reasons, a complex and problematic business. One of the main issues involved in an understanding of the Roman political system is, as we will see, an assessment of how far there was significant participation on the part of the ordinary citizens of Rome (and beyond). The fact that the texts are generated by a social elite makes it difficult, if not impossible, to view politics from the point of view of the 'man in the street' or fully to understand the economic and social pressures by which the population of the city was constrained.

The writings of Cicero, who himself was a leading protagonist from the 70s BC until his death in 43, provide a vital source of information. His letters, speeches and philosophical works (for which see T. Wiedemann's *Cicero and the End of the Roman Republic* in this series) contain a wealth of allusion to contemporary political structures and events. The difficulty is that Cicero, who was intimately involved in the events to which he refers, is seldom (if ever) a neutral commentator. On the one hand he had his own clearly defined political ideals, and a strong attachment to the traditions of the Republic; on the other he frequently spoke in defence of individuals involved in controversial and highly politically charged trials, and had both to persuade an audience and to present his client's activities in the best possible light. The speeches Cicero delivered as consul in 63 BC may well, like many other of his speeches, have been written up afterwards to glorify his own activities in suppressing Catiline's conspiracy, which had become increasingly controversial in the following years.

Other versions of the history of these years are provided by the historian Sallust, who served as a tribune of the plebs and praetor, and was himself expelled from the Senate in 52 BC, and by three authors writing in Greek in the second and third centuries AD: Appian, Cassius Dio and Plutarch. We rely on the first two of these writers for narrative accounts of the last years of the Republic (although written well after the events, and within the rather different political and ideological context of the Empire), and the. latter for biographical portraits of leading individuals involved in Roman politics. As a result, the focus of historical attention has traditionally been more often on the individual than on the system as a whole. It should also not be forgotten that, although the last thirty years of the Republic represent perhaps the best documented period in antiquity, events of less than a century earlier are much more obscure: there is a particular gap in our knowledge between 167 BC (when Livy's narrative breaks off) and 133 BC (when Appian's begins). Increased attention to non-literary sources such as coins, inscriptions (especially those preserving the texts of laws, or charters of communities in the provinces) and archaeology have provided a valuable corrective to the difficulties generated by the nature of the surviving literary record. However, the unique level of detail provided by that record, together with its high literary quality, have surely contributed to the particular fascination of the study of later republican politics.

The topography of Rome

Just as the interpretation of the literary sources for the late Republic is a complex operation, so the understanding of the urban topography of the city of Rome is not at all straightforward. One particular problem is that the imperial – and still more the republican – remains are buried many metres below modern street level, beneath the buildings of the mediaeval, renaissance, nineteenth-century and modern phases of the city (Fig. 2). As a result, excavation of the buildings of republican Rome is a difficult, though not impossible, business. Recent investigations on the slopes of the Palatine have successfully revealed a series of houses of early republican date located on top of the remains of an eighth-century BC fortification wall. The archaeology of the republican city is therefore something that is well understood in certain closely investigated areas of the city, but more obscure elsewhere. Several of the areas of central Rome most important in political terms, such as the Comitium (the open space for political meetings located in front of the Senate House) and the Forum, were investigated as part of the extensive researches undertaken at the very end of the nineteenth century by the archaeologist Giacomo Boni. The interpretation of the data recovered by Boni was the object of heated debate even at the time of the discoveries. By contrast, the ancient Campus Martius was in the mediaeval period the most densely occupied area of the city of Rome, so reconstructing how it was laid out in antiquity has been a particularly difficult and gradual process.

Scholars working on the historical topography of Rome are able to draw on a wealth of (often problematical) evidence in addition to the data provided by excavation. Often the study of the existing buildings of the city – or those which are recorded as having existed but are no longer visible – can also cast light on the antiquities that lie beneath the city's streets. In the Campus Martius, for example, the outlines of the Theatre

Fig 2 View of the Campus Martius. The photograph illustrates the density of mediaeval, renaissance and modern building in the area, and the difficulties involved in reconstructing the topography of the Campus in antiquity. The low dome in the centre of the photograph is that of Hadrian's Pantheon (2nd century AD).

and Portico of Pompey, constructed in 55 BC, are reflected in the street-grid of the mediaeval buildings around the Campo de' Fiori, while renaissance drawings of ancient remains (or photography from the nineteenth and early twentieth centuries) have often provided the only evidence of monuments in the city which have subsequently disappeared. Some ancient buildings – for example, the late antique Senate House (see Fig. 3, page 13), and the Temple of Portunus in the Forum Boarium – have survived from antiquity in a good state of preservation as a result of having been converted into churches in the early mediaeval period.

Literary texts, coupled with archaeological evidence, are of particular importance for the reconstruction of the changing layout of the city in the republican period; the construction of public buildings like temples or basilicas was considered worthy of being recorded in the pontifical annals, which Livy's sources may have used as a basis of their narrative. Temples and other monuments were, from the latter part of the second century BC onwards, often used as images on coins and, although the extent to which these images can be considered accurate representations of the physical monuments is sometimes doubtful, the coins can provide useful chronological evidence. The Marble Plan of Rome, which was displayed in the Forum of Peace early in the third century AD, is an invaluable source of information about the appearance of the city in the imperial period, although sadly only about ten per cent of the whole document now survives. Of course, significant changes had already occurred in the organisation and layout of the city between the end of the Republic and the third century; yet it remains a document of unique importance for the reconstruction of the topography of Rome.

The development of knowledge over the past few decades has led to significant leaps forward in our understanding of the urban landscape in antiquity. Until the 1930s, for example, it was firmly believed that the Saepta Iulia, the marble-built enclosure projected by Julius Caesar and eventually constructed by Augustus' close associate Marcus Agrippa on the Campus Martius as a meeting place for the voting assemblies, was located along the Via Flaminia which led northwards from the monumental centre of Rome. Careful comparison by the topographer Guglielmo Gatti of the fragment of the Marble Plan, which purported to depict the Saepta Iulia, with remains of a major building excavated next to the Tiber below the Aventine Hill revealed that the fragment did not depict the Saepta at all, but the Porticus Aemilia, a monumental warehouse on the opposite side of Rome. The Saepta was then relocated to its now generally accepted position just to the east of the Pantheon, on the basis of two other fragments of the Plan. Some 25 years later the same scholar noted a join between two fragments of the Marble Plan which showed that the Circus Flaminius (not an arena for chariot-racing like the Circus Maximus but an open space, laid out in 221 BC by the tribune C. Flaminius along the route of the triumphal procession) was to be located to the south of the Porticus Octaviae and Porticus Philippi, some 200 metres south of the location in which it had traditionally been placed. Very recently, the archaeologist Paolo Carafa has persuasively argued in a radical new study (see p. 14) that the Comitium was triangular in shape rather than being circular (as usually believed); and that the Senate House was located on a rock outcrop ten metres above the Comitium, instead of being immediately adjacent to it. Although in general the process of reconstructing the topography of the city is slow and painstaking, the discovery of a new piece of archaeological or other evidence, or a brilliant new reading of the existing data, can lead to dramatic reappraisal of traditional views on the locations of major monuments.

Chapter 3

The Roman political system in outline

In his account of Rome's rise to power over the Mediterranean between 264 BC, when the First Punic War between Rome and Carthage broke out, and the defeat of both Carthage and Corinth in 146 BC, Polybius (a Greek writer who came to Rome as a hostage in the 160s and became close to leading Roman families such as the Scipios) provided a detailed analytical account of the Roman political system. This drew on the traditional vocabulary of Greek thought which categorised political systems as monarchy (rule by a king), aristocracy (rule by the 'best men' – usually taken to mean 'the wealthy') and democracy (rule by the people). Polybius observed that:

> There were three elements controlling the state...and everything was organised and administered so equally and so fittingly through these elements that no-one – not even one of the Romans themselves – could say definitively whether the whole constitution was aristocratic, democratic or monarchical. This was reasonable, for if one looked at the powers of the consuls, the system seemed completely monarchical and regal; if one looked at those of the senate, however, it appeared to be aristocratic; and if one examined the powers of the masses, it seemed clearly to be democratic. (POLYBIUS 6.11)

This chapter outlines the key features of this complex web of political institutions, and in particular the combination of senate, popular assemblies and magistracies, which Polybius so admired.

The popular assemblies

The people of republican Rome – the 'democratic' element in Polybius' analysis – had no fewer than four popular assemblies, each with its own distinctive membership, organisation, and responsibilities, but they all shared the characteristic that voting was conducted not on a basis of 'one man one vote' (participation, as was normal in ancient political systems, was limited to male citizens, in the case of Rome those over the age of

17 years), but according to the principle of group voting. The groups in each assembly were differently structured, and might be organised according to the wealth or place of origin of the voters, but the principle was the same: the members of the group would vote on a legislative proposal or between candidates in an election, reach a majority decision, and the group's collective vote would then be registered for or against the proposal, or for a particular candidate or candidates. Voting by the groups would take place until a majority in favour of or against the proposal was achieved, or sufficient groups had voted for a clear decision to be made between the several candidates contesting office – at which point the meeting of the assembly would have reached its conclusion. The system is more like that of the conventions which elect candidates for the office of President of the United States than the process by which Members of Parliament in the United Kingdom are (currently) elected by their constituents in the so- called 'first past the post' electoral system, in which the candidate with the most individual votes is declared elected.

The comitia curiata

The different ways in which the different groups were defined was of major importance. The oldest of the four assemblies was the *comitia curiata*. This was composed of thirty *curiae*, subdivisions of the most archaic tribes of Rome, the Ramnes, Tities and Luceres. By the late Republic, its importance for practical politics was minimal, though it still had formally to ratify the election of magistrates by the other assemblies (see below). It might also be summoned to deal with matters concerning wills, adoptions, and cases in which members of the patrician class voluntarily relinquished their status and became plebeians instead. This famously happened in the case of P. Clodius Pulcher, who in 59 BC abandoned his prestigious status of patrician (there were a limited number of patrician families, who were descended from the earliest aristocracy of Rome and inherited privileged status) and became a plebeian in order to stand for election as a tribune of the plebs. In our period, the thirty *curiae* were generally represented by thirty lictors, one for each *curia*.

Much more important were the three remaining assemblies, the *comitia centuriata*, the *comitia tributa* and the *concilium plebis*.

The comitia centuriata

The organisation of the *comitia centuriata* was attributed to Servius Tullius, the penultimate king of Rome, in the mid-sixth century BC. The assembly was responsible for electing senior magistrates (censors, consuls and praetors: see below), and for declarations of war and peace. It also had the power to pass laws, though from the third century onwards these were usually brought to the other two main assemblies; one notable exception was the law passed in 57 BC to secure Cicero's return from the exile into which he had been sent following the execution of the Catilinarian conspirators in 63 BC. Livy and Dionysius of Halicarnassus (a Greek critic and historian writing in the Augustan period) both provide detailed accounts of the assembly – which are the basis for modern writers' reconstructions of how it worked; their explanations show how the assembly was related to arrangements for the Roman army. Both the assembly and the army were organised in an overtly hierarchical way. The type of military duties citizens were obliged to perform in the Roman army, as in other armies in the Classical world, depended on their financial status – the wealthiest served as cavalry, the poorest as slingers, for example – and the political privileges granted to citizens were similarly defined by the extent of their wealth. Voting units were called centuries, like the units in the Roman army under the command of a centurion, but with the difference that whereas army units were of a standard size, the centuries in the *comitia centuriata* must have varied in size considerably, according to the number of individual citizens belonging to a particular 'wealth band'.

The complex arrangement of the *comitia centuriata* appears to have undergone some reorganisation, probably in the late third century BC, which had an effect on the number of voting centuries allocated to each class, and changed the order of voting. It consisted of 193 centuries in total. The wealthiest citizens, those who in the late republican period possessed more than 400,000 sesterces, and so belonged to the equestrian order (the cavalry, in notional terms), were allocated to 18 centuries. The next wealthiest group, Class I, were allocated to 80 centuries under Servius Tullius' arrangements, but this seems to have been reduced to 70 centuries after the reform mentioned above. The members of Classes II-V were allocated to 90 centuries at first, then to 100; specialist army units including engineers, servants, trumpeters and buglers to four centuries; while that mass of poorer citizens who had very little wealth were lumped together in a single century and called *capite censi* ('counted by heads alone', in other words not possessing any significant wealth) or *proletarii* ('capable only of producing children for the state').

The arrangements can be tabulated as follows:

	Servius Tullius' arrangements	Post 3rd c. BC reorganisation
equites	18	18
Class I	80	70
Classes II-V	90 ⎫	
Buglers etc	4 ⎬	105
capite censi	1 ⎭	
Total	193	193

Under the original arrangements, therefore, the *equites* and members of Class I, if they voted together, gained a majority of the centuries in the assembly; even under the revised arrangements, only a few centuries in Class II had to vote with their superiors to obtain a majority. Furthermore, until the third-century BC reform the *equites* voted first and their decision, when announced, gave a symbolic lead to the assembly. Afterwards, however, one of the centuries from Class I was selected by lot as the *centuria praerogativa*, which would announce its vote first. The remaining centuries would then vote in order of seniority, beginning with those in Class I, until a proposal had been approved by a majority of the centuries – at which point the assembly would be brought to an end.

The *comitia centuriata* met outside the *pomerium* (the ritual boundary of the city), in the *ovile* or Saepta (voting enclosure) on the Campus Martius, which was also where the census was taken and where the army assembled before a triumphal procession (see Chapter 4). Following an ancient ritual, a red flag was flown on the Janiculum Hill when the assembly was in session. The origin of this strange custom was that in earliest times, the Janiculum, located on the other side of the Tiber from the main part of the city, was continually under threat from Rome's Etruscan neighbours. A garrison therefore occupied the hill when the assembly was meeting to warn of possible Etruscan attacks, which would be signalled by the lowering of the flag, at which the assembly would be dissolved and the Romans prepared to resist the attack on the city. In 63 BC the flag was lowered in order to bring to a premature end an extraordinary meeting of the assembly which had been convened to try C. Rabirius on a charge of *perduellio* (high treason) under an archaic procedure; as the assembly was abandoned, Rabirius was released. Dio tells us that the practice of flying the flag continued until his own time (the early third century AD) 'on account of reverence for tradition' (DIO 37. 28). Until the time of Augustus there seems to have been little in the way of permanent structures on the site, temporary enclosures being set up to contain the voters. A building known as the Villa Publica served as the administrative centre for the elections.

The comitia tributa *and* concilium plebis

The *comitia tributa* and *concilium plebis* were in many ways very similar to each other, with the significant difference that the membership of the *concilium plebis* seems to have consisted only of plebeians, whereas the *comitia tributa* contained both plebeians and patricians – though the numbers of the latter were very much smaller than those of the former. The *comitia tributa* elected quaestors, curule aediles, and other junior magistrates, and had the power to pass laws; so too, after the passing of the Lex Hortensia in 287 BC, did the assembly of the plebs, the *concilium plebis*, which also elected the plebeian magistrates – the plebeian aediles and the tribunes. Both assemblies were formally organised on a regional (rather than financially hierarchical) basis; by 241 BC there were 35 tribes (31 rural and 4 urban), a number which had gradually been built up as Rome's territory expanded and more Italians gained Roman citizenship. Again, the members of the different tribes voted together – simultaneously in the case of elections, one after the other in the case of legislation – and the tribe's collective vote was then registered in favour of a proposal or candidate.

Voting

In all three major assemblies voting was originally oral (voters declared their preference orally to the tellers), but from 139 BC, in the case of elections, and 131 BC, in the case of legislative assemblies, the secret ballot was introduced: at legislative meetings voters deposited in the ballot-box tablets inscribed 'V' (i.e. *uti rogas*, meaning 'as you request') if they were in favour of the proposal, or 'A' (i.e. *antiquo*, meaning 'as things were before') if they were against the measure. In elections, candidates wrote the initials of candidates they supported on a wax tablet. The introduction of the secret ballot was regarded with disapproving hindsight by conservative senators such as Cicero (whose own grandfather had been vehemently opposed to the new system being introduced in his home town of Arpinum): 'who does not know that the laws providing for a secret ballot have removed all the authority of the best citizens (*optimates*)?' (*On the Laws* 3. 34). Thus this new device can be regarded as a move in the direction of democratic practice; it would presumably have made influencing and intimidating voters less easy than with oral declarations of preference – though doubtless not impossible. A measure implemented in 119 BC to narrow the *pontes* ('bridges') across which voters passed before casting their ballot must similarly have been intended to discourage intimidation.

The meeting-places

Where these assemblies met depended on whether the gathering had been summoned in order to pass legislation or to vote in elections. There were several locations in the city which were particularly associated with popular politics, notably the Comitium, the Campus Martius, the Capitol,

Fig 3 The Forum Romanum seen from the Palatine Hill. The brick building to the right of the photograph is the late antique Senate House.

and the Circus Flaminius. The *comitia centuriata* (because of its identity with the Roman state in arms) had to meet outside the *pomerium*, as we have seen. The *comitia tributa*, by contrast, although it met in the Campus for electoral business (because all the tribes voted simultaneously, and more space was required), would, when meeting for legislative purposes, assemble in the more limited space available on the Capitol or in the Forum. Frontinus (the first century AD writer, consul and former governor of Britain) quotes the Lex Quinctia of 9 BC on aqueducts, which illustrates not only where the legislation was passed, but also that the first tribe to vote, and the first individual to vote, were carefully recorded:

> T. Quinctius Crispinus the consul...duly consulted the people and the people duly passed a resolution in the Forum, in front of the Rostra of the Temple of the Divine Julius Caesar, on the thirtieth day of June. The Sergian tribe was the first to vote. On behalf of the tribe, Sex. Virro, son of Lucius, cast his vote first.
> (FRONTINUS, *On Aqueducts* 2.129)

From Comitium to Forum

However, it was the Comitium which was the archetypal location for popular politics. This was located in front of the Senate House or Curia, and together Curia and Comitium formed a model of political space which was adopted wherever the Romans built Latin colonies, reflecting their self-governing status. Near the Curia stood the Tribunal of the praetors, where legal judgements were enacted, and the benches of the tribunes, ready to intervene when the rights of individual Roman citizens were under threat. Not far away were the Tarpeian Rock and the Carcer, places of execution. Located opposite was the Graecostasis (occupied by visiting ambassadors waiting to address members of the senate) and the Rostra, from which magistrates spoke to the Roman people with the Senate House forming a backdrop. The key elements of the Roman state – senate, popular assembly, magistrates – together with the tribunes of the plebs, and the locations most closely linked with state punishment, were symbolised by a complex of monuments gathered together in a small area adjacent to the Forum (Fig. 4).

The Comitium is thought to have held somewhere between 3,000 and 6,000 people, depending whether we imagine it to be triangular (following Carafa's reconstruction; see Chapter 2) or circular (as conventionally believed). By the mid-second century it had clearly become too small as a location for meetings of the popular assembly. The solution adopted was to transfer the popular meetings to the main body of the Forum. Voting assemblies were moved from the Comitium to the Forum by C. Licinius Crassus, tribune in 145 BC; and Gaius Gracchus, tribune some 20 years later, moved *contiones* (informal meetings at which magistrates would address the People) to the same location 'in a way changing the constitution from an aristocracy to a democracy' (PLUTARCH, *Gaius Gracchus* 5). Orators would now stand with their back to the Senate House, facing the crowd assembled in the Forum – a reform which evidently caused considerable offence in conservative circles.

Views differ among experts on Roman topography as to when the Comitium ceased to be an identifiable political space: the archaeologist

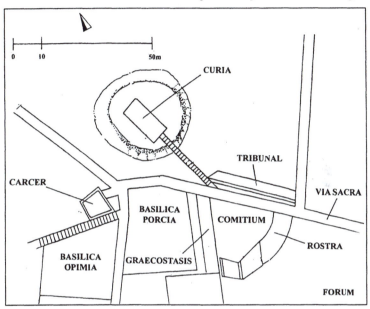

Fig 4 The Curia and the Comitium in the late Republic (based on Carafa's reconstruction).

Filippo Coarelli, in his important study of the Forum, argues that when Sulla expanded the membership of the senate to 600 (see p. 21) and built a new Curia to house them, the new building in part extended over the land formerly occupied by the adjacent Comitium. For Carafa, the difference in level between Curia and Comitium means the project had little impact on the latter. It is very clear, however, that by the time of Augustus the Comitium was no longer of any political significance and had virtually disappeared: Julius Caesar had relocated the Rostra on an entirely new alignment on the central axis of the Forum.

An election on the Campus Martius

A detailed account of an electoral meeting of the *comitia tributa* is to be found in the unlikely setting of the third book of the treatise *On*

Agriculture by Varro, the distinguished first-century BC Roman scholar. Although it deals largely with the apparently mundane subject of how to keep birds and small animals on a farm, the treatise is written in the dialogue form originally associated with the Greek philosopher Plato, complete with a variety of entertaining incidents which break up the presentation of Varro's views on the rearing of fowl. The dialogue is set at the election of aediles (i.e. in the *comitia tributa*), on the Campus Martius, probably to be dated to 54 or 50 BC. Varro and a senator, Q. Axius, who belong to the same tribe, cast their votes and then decide to wait under the shade of the Villa Publica until the conclusion of the voting so they can accompany their favoured candidate home at the end of the day. In the Villa Publica they encounter Appius Claudius the *augur*, and several friends, all of whom have *cognomina* taken from birds. (As well as their family name, e.g. Tullius, and their personal name, e.g. Marcus, Romans frequently had a third name, or *cognomen*, which often referred to a physical peculiarity or was otherwise satirical in tone). Here are met Cornelius Merula 'the Blackbird', Fircellius Pavo 'the Peacock', Minucius Pica 'the Magpie', and Petronius Passer 'the Sparrow', which allows Varro to make a series of punning references throughout the dialogue. Jokingly, Axius asks Appius:

> Will you let us come into your aviary, where you are sitting among the birds? (VARRO, *On Agriculture* 3.2.2)

Axius and Appius are invited to join the party, and a discussion follows about the Villa Publica 'which is suitable for conducting public business, where the cohorts assemble when summoned for a levy by the consul, where they display their arms, and where the censors admit the populace for the census' (3.2.4). This then leads on to a more general debate about villas and the rearing of birds and small animals – such as dormice and snails – for the market at Rome. The discussion concentrates on birds, but is then disrupted by a shouting in the Campus. 'We veterans of the assemblies were not surprised when this happened, because of the passionate enthusiasm of those supporting the candidates', comments Varro. Pantuleius Parra 'the Owl' arrives and explains that, while the counting of the votes was taking place, a man had been caught improperly placing ballots in the ballot-box, and had been taken away to the consul 'by the supporters of the other candidates' (3.5.18). Fircellius Pavo gets up and leaves, since it is a supporter of his candidate who has been arrested. 'You may speak freely about peacocks, now that Fircellius is gone' says Axius (3.6.1), and the discussion continues on that theme.

Another interruption occurs when Appius, as *augur*, is called away: some pigeons fly into the villa, and the conversation moves off in that direction, turning then to the rearing and care of chickens and ducks, snails, dormice, and bees, before Pavo returns explaining that the result of the voting is about to be announced. More noise is heard and Varro and Axius see their candidate, successfully elected, wearing the purple-bordered toga of the aedile. 'We go up to him and congratulate him, and accompany him to the Capitol' (3.17.9).

In a light-hearted way, Varro's dialogue illustrates many of the most notable features of Roman elections: the physical setting, the voting procedure, the substantial length of time it took for the voting to be concluded, the concern for religious observance, and the abuses that might be practised on election-day.

Participation and its limitations

How far did the Roman political system allow its citizens to make a significant contribution to decision-making, or even to take part in politics in a meaningful way? Slaves, non-citizens and female citizens were all excluded from the political process, as was normal in ancient states; and many features of the Roman system can be seen as highly undemocratic, especially by comparison with the Athenian democracy of the fifth century BC. In particular, political activity could only take place within the city of Rome itself. Under the early Republic, the distances citizens had to travel to Rome might have been comparatively small, as the area under Roman control was limited; however, by the mid-first century BC, Roman citizens were scattered all over Italy, up to 500 km. from Rome (and even beyond), but they still had to travel to the capital if they wanted to vote on legislation, take part in elections, or attend political meetings. A poorly attested reform introduced by Augustus, allowing councillors of Italian towns to vote in their own community and the ballots then to be taken for counting at Rome, suggests a later awareness of the problem. The dates of many assemblies were irregular (apart from those of elections which during the late Republic took place at fixed times in the year, normally in July), as they could be summoned by a magistrate with three weeks' notice; and there was always the risk that ill omens might be observed which would cause the postponement of the meeting. When a meeting of the *comitia* was held, the participants voted but there was no discussion, nor was it possible to amend a proposal; this took place in the senate at the (usual) preliminary debate on the proposal. Instead, the magistrates would address the people on a legislative proposal at a *contio*, a preliminary meeting of the people, though again the ordinary citizens would not have the opportunity to discuss the measure in public themselves. The protagonists in Roman politics were invariably members of the social and economic elite, who had to surpass a wealth qualification (400,000 sesterces under the Republic, as we have seen) to be eligible to stand for office.

The different patterns of organisation within the various assemblies meant that the nature of popular involvement varied significantly between them. The hierarchical and fundamentally undemocratic nature of the *comitia centuriata* was clear to ancient writers like Livy, who observed that 'gradations were introduced, so that no-one should seem to be excluded from the right to vote, but all the power should remain with the leading men in the state' (LIVY 1.43.10). For politicians like Cicero, this was one of its best features.

> When the populace is organised according to wealth, rank and age, it brings sounder judgement to bear than when summoned in an unclassified fashion in the tribal assembly.
>
> (CICERO, *On the Laws* 3.44.)

Dionysius of Halicarnassus, who claimed to have witnessed meetings of the assembly himself, did however observe that the *comitia centuriata* had become more democratic since the time of Servius Tullius, presumably referring to the late third-century reorganisation of the voting centuries in the classes and the selection by lot of the *centuria praerogativa* to replace the leading role of the *equites*. One central issue which is still the subject of debate is the property qualification for registration in Class I, for which estimates range from 25,000 to 100,000 sesterces. In view of the consensus of the ancient sources that the *comitia centuriata* was indeed an elitist body, a figure at the higher end of this range is more likely; but if a lower figure were preferred, the occupants of Class I might be regarded as being of rather lower social status than often assumed, and the assembly correspondingly more 'democratic'. In any case, if an election was closely contested, it was quite possible that the vote might be decided by one of the lower centuries – even the *capite censi*.

The *concilium plebis* and *comitia tributa* were less overtly hierarchical in structure than the *comitia centuriata*; indeed it is quite striking that within the tribal units in these assemblies the votes of the poorest and wealthiest citizens alike were accorded equal value. These assemblies too were liable to their own biases. In particular, the distribution of citizens among the voting tribes was contentious, because the significance of an individual's vote in the tribal assemblies would depend not only on how many people were registered in a particular tribe overall, but how many of them might reasonably be expected to appear in person to vote. For example, freedmen (ex-slaves) granted Roman citizenship were enrolled in the four urban tribes, whether or not they actually lived in the city of Rome, and this had the effect of diminishing their political importance because the urban tribes contained very large numbers of citizens, many of whom lived in the city itself, and so would readily be able to attend political meetings. Several (unsuccessful) attempts were made to register freedmen in all the tribes, and P. Clodius was planning another measure on these lines at the time of his death in 52 BC. In the same way, after the Social War (91-87 BC), when all Italians were granted the Roman citizenship, there was considerable wrangling over the tribes to which the newly enfranchised Italians should be allocated. During the last years of the Republic, some of the rural tribes seem to have had many fewer members than others: the Romilia (which consisted almost entirely of the inhabitants of Sora, a former Latin colony in the valley of the Liri, south-east of Rome), and Pupinia (primarily comprising the inhabitants of Sarsina in Umbria) were very sparsely populated. As a result their members had a disproportionate influence in the vote, and must have been specially cultivated by those who were standing for election in the tribal assembly.

How many people voted at the assemblies, and how far those living in the countryside attended on a regular basis is hard to determine. The capacity of the Comitium is, as noted above, believed to be have been somewhere between 3,000 and 6,000, while it has been estimated (on the basis of the dimensions of the Saepta of imperial date) that the maximum number of voters who could have packed into the voting enclosures on the Campus Martius was somewhere between 50,000 and 70,000. On the other hand, it seems unlikely that every vote would have been equally vigorously contested, so we may imagine that on some occasions there were many fewer voters present. Indeed provision existed for a presiding magistrate to select five voters to represent a tribe if it would otherwise have been unrepresented. We hear of particular occasions when large numbers of voters came into Rome to vote for a particular measure: on the occasion when C. Gracchus was elected tribune for the year 123 BC in the *concilium plebis*, Plutarch tells us that:

> such a vast multitude came together into the city from Italy to take part in the election that for many there was no accommodation, and since the Campus Martius could not contain the whole crowd, they shouted in support from the rooftops.

Plutarch goes on to note that despite this display of popular support Gracchus was elected only in fourth place out of the ten vacancies for tribune (PLUTARCH, *Gaius Gracchus* 3). Cicero similarly refers to the extensive crowds that flocked to Rome to vote for his return from exile in 57 BC. But it is unclear how typical these episodes were. We might expect that, given the distances involved, comparatively few people from outside the city would have been able to attend assembly meetings in Rome on a regular basis. A very popular proposal perceived to be of benefit to the mass of the country-dwellers, or the potential election of a charismatic figure like C. Gracchus, might have brought in a large crowd. In the same way, there seems to have been an energetic and co-ordinated campaign to muster rural support on behalf of Cicero from across Italy. An individual with strong connections in Italy may have made special efforts to gather in supporters from a distance. In such circumstances, financial and practical help may have been offered to the rank-and-file voters attending the *comitia* to compensate for the practical difficulties involved in attending the vote. While it was easier for the people of Rome than the country-dwellers to attend the assemblies, there were only four tribes formally designated for the urban population, as opposed to the 31 rural tribes. However, since no effective censuses took place between 70 BC and the time of Augustus, it is likely that few immigrants to the city from the countryside were actually registered in the urban tribes in that period, and many must have remained in their original rural tribes despite living in the city. They would thus have been particularly influential in the voting of the tribal assembly in the latter years of the Republic.

A 'democratic' element?

Despite the various generally accepted restrictions on widespread popular participation in political decision-making at Rome, there has in recent years been considerable interest in what we might for convenience call the 'democratic' features of Roman politics, in particular as a result of an influential series of publications by Fergus Millar, the present occupant of the Camden chair of Ancient History at Oxford. This approach has drawn attention to the weight placed on the 'democratic' element in the Roman state in the account given by Polybius of the Roman constitution. It is the people, says Polybius, who:

> confer office on those who deserve it, the most glorious reward for virtue in the state; they also have the power to decide on the approval or rejection of laws, and, most important of all, they debate issues of war and peace.   (POLYBIUS 6.14)

Why, it might be asked, does Polybius, who knew Rome and Roman politics well, make so much of the 'democratic' element if it was clearly of minimal importance, as much modern literature suggests? Likewise, it is clear from literary accounts that elections were in practice seldom foregone conclusions, and were energetically contested by the participants (as discussed in Chapter 5). Candidates canvassed voters and addressed meetings of the people, entertained them, bribed them and in some cases intimidated them; again one has to ask why, if the outcome of the elections was easily predictable. Why, similarly, did the consuls hold meetings of the people, such as those in 63 BC (versions of which are preserved as Cicero's Second and Third *Speeches against Catiline*) at which Cicero recounted to the people the departure of Catiline from Rome, and the arrest of his fellow-conspirators, if the people had little real political power? An understanding of the relationship between the politically ambitious members of the aristocracy and the people is clearly vital to an understanding of the nature of the Roman political process, as discussed in Chapter 4. I shall be arguing that there was indeed a significant element of popular participation in the elections, in the sense that the votes of ordinary Romans could be decisive where an election was strongly contested, and as a result the political elite could not afford to ignore them; in fact, the participation of supporters, associates and clients was a central element in the public activities of the elite generally. The practical difficulties of participation meant, however, that those involved in the voting assemblies should not be seen as in any sense representative of the Roman citizen body as a whole, a weakness that was to contribute to the eventual collapse of the political system of the Republic.

The senate

The senate (which formed the 'aristocratic' element in Polybius' analysis) was both the central decision-making body and the repository of collected political wisdom in the Roman state, though the nature of its authority and its precise constitutional status was always somewhat obscure. Originally the senate seems to have been conceived of as an advisory council of 100 members, providing guidance for, and appointed by, the Kings, but it subsequently became a larger, more permanent body which numbered 300 members, and was doubled in size after Sulla's reforms in 81 BC. During the chaotic conditions of the Civil Wars of the late first century BC it grew to nearly a thousand members before being reduced to 600 again as part of reforms initiated by Augustus. In the regal period recruitment was apparently based on the favour of a particular king, but later the members were selected by the censors, who were appointed every five years to conduct the census of Roman citizens and to review the roll of the senate. It seems that those recruited were drawn largely from the ranks of ex-magistrates. Sulla, as well as increasing the size of the senate, established that those elected to the quaestorship should automatically become senators. Subsequently, therefore, the senate was indirectly elected by the popular assembly. Membership, once achieved, was for life, although the censors retained the right to expel members of that body for immoral conduct, or if they fell below the property qualification required for membership.

Polybius (6.13) describes the main areas of the senate's responsibilities, which he sees as primarily concerned with the spheres of finance and 'foreign affairs': controlling the expenditure proposed by the censors on public works, dealing with cases of arbitration within Italy, and receiving and responding to embassies sent by other states. In addition, the senate also had religious responsibilities – deciding the state's response to omens, portents and other untoward religious occurrences. It also acted (in its traditional role) as a body which could provide magistrates, most specifically the consuls, with advice and guidance. In practice, if not in theory (for only the Roman People could make laws) the senate was the main governing body at Rome; it was highly unusual for major decisions or legislation to take place without prior detailed consideration by that body. The senate had to be summoned by a magistrate, usually a consul, and discussion was initiated in the form of a magistrate's proposal. The debate then took place in order of seniority, with (from Sulla's time onwards) ex-consuls, the most distinguished senators, speaking first, followed by ex-praetors and other former magistrates according to the offices they had held.

The normal meeting-place for the senate of the Republic was the purpose-built Senate House or Curia, which stood on the edge of the Roman Forum, on a low hill above the Comitium. Because of its importance as a body which would decide on matters pertaining to religion, the senate was obliged to meet in a *templum*, a space formally delimited by the *augurs* as a sacred precinct. The Curia was such a *templum*; otherwise the senate might meet in a temple (in our sense), as happened quite frequently. The first meeting of each year took place in the Temple of Jupiter Capitolinus, as did meetings at which warfare was to be discussed. Other temples were chosen for meetings for either practical or symbolic reasons. For example on 8 November 63 BC, when Cicero summoned the senators to denounce Catiline's plots, they met in the Temple of Jupiter Stator. The precise location of this temple is not firmly known, but it seems to have been situated on the slopes leading down to the Forum from the Palatine. The site was easily defensible (a bodyguard of *equites* was stationed around the temple) but it also had strong ideological associations, in that the temple had originally been established by Romulus, who appealed to 'Jupiter, Stayer of Flight' to stop the Romans being routed in an early battle with the Sabines. The temple therefore symbolised Roman firmness in the face of enemy threats. In a similar way, the meetings at which the evidence making clear the guilt of the conspirators was revealed (on 3 December), and at which the senators decided the fate of the conspirators (on 5 December), were held in the Temple of Concord, on the slopes of the Capitoline hill. Again, this was a choice justifiable both in practical and symbolic terms. It was close to the *carcer* – Rome's place of execution, to which Catiline's supporters were dragged from the houses of leading magistrates where they had been imprisoned. In addition, the Temple of Concord had strong ideological associations with the conservative viewpoint in the Roman state: it had been rebuilt by L. Opimius, who led the mob that put C. Gracchus to death in 121 BC, an irony not lost on contemporaries. Plutarch noted that someone wrote on the temple: 'a deed of discord produces a Temple of Concord' (*Gaius Gracchus* 17). The conspirators must have realised their fate was sealed when they learnt where the senate was to discuss their case.

Occasionally the senate would need to meet outside the *pomerium*, in particular when it had to receive generals still in command of armies, who were not allowed to cross the ritual boundary of the city, or those ambassadors who were not authorised to enter the city. On these occasions it would often meet at the Temple of Apollo or that of Bellona, both of which were located between the Capitol and the Circus Flaminius.

The Curia, though, was the building most closely associated with the senate, and its history reflects the turbulent history of the body which met within it. The original structure, the 'Curia Hostilia', was replaced in around 80 BC by a new building constructed by Sulla to house his enlarged senate. This was destroyed in 52 BC (together with the neighbouring Basilica Porcia), when the supporters of Clodius – who had been killed in a fight on the Appian Way with his rival Milo and his supporters – carried their hero's body into the Senate House and cremated it there, using benches, tables and books of records to make a pyre. Sulla's Senate House was restored by his son Faustus Sulla, but in 46 BC this was demolished to make way for a Temple of Felicitas, and a new Curia constructed on the same alignment as the Forum of Julius Caesar, which was completed in 29 BC. The Curia built by the Emperor Diocletian early in the fourth century AD – and still visible in the Forum – stands on the same site (see Fig. 3, p. 13).

The magistrates

Since access to the senate was in the late Republic determined entirely by whether an individual had held a magistracy, elections to magistracies were clearly an important element in the creation of the political elite; and those holding the most prestigious offices of state, the consulship and the censorship, were in each case appointed by means of election. Only those who owned wealth of 400,000 sesterces or more, members of the equestrian order, were allowed to stand for magisterial office. (By way of comparison, the annual earnings of an ordinary soldier under the late Republic were about 450 sesterces, until this figure was doubled by Julius Caesar.) Candidates for each magistracy were elected by a particular assembly: the *comitia centuriata* in the case of consuls, praetors and censors; the *comitia tributa* in the case of curule aediles, quaestors, and other more junior magistrates; the *concilium plebis* in the case of plebeian aediles and tribunes. Elections normally took place in July. Two consuls were elected each year and together acted as chief magistrates of the state; the prestige of the office is shown by the fact that the formal designation of the year in which they served was 'in the consulship of X and Y'. As well as summoning the senate and acting as its executive officers, the consuls took command of the army in the field, although after Sulla it was common for the consuls to remain in Rome for much of their term of office and then take up a military command. Originally the consuls had responsibility for jurisdiction too, but the institution of the praetorship in 367 BC, and then the creation of a second praetor in 242, largely freed them from that duty. Two more praetorships were instituted in 227 to govern Sicily and Sardinia and an additional two in 197 to run the recently acquired territories in Spain. The number was increased to eight by Sulla; the praetors, like the consuls, tended to remain in Rome during their term of office and then take up a provincial command as propraetor afterwards. Four aediles, two curule aediles elected by the *comitia tributa* and two plebeian aediles elected by the *concilium plebis*, had responsibility for the day-to-day running of the city of Rome, in particular maintenance of roads and buildings, organisation of the games and care of the corn supply. The tribunes of the plebs – originally established in the context of the conflicts of the early Republic between patricians and plebeians – continued to play a major role in the politics of the late Republic, despite a concerted attempt by Sulla to reduce their influence. They presided over the *concilium plebis* (which since 287 BC had had the right to pass laws) and could veto the proposals of other magistrates as well as assist individual plebeians. Tribunes frequently put forward proposals connected with the political rights and the living conditions of the Roman plebs, for example, measures concerned with voting procedures, land distribution and the corn supply, but they were also well placed to bring forward legislation in the *concilium plebis* in support of political allies. Quaestors originally acted as the assistants of the consuls in financial affairs, and continued to assist magistrates outside Rome. There were two each year in the early Republic, and by the beginning of the second century there were eight, the number being raised to twenty by Sulla as part of his reform of the senate. Winning the quaestorship brought with it membership of the senate, so the elections to this office were of particular importance.

The problem of senatorial openness

Ancient writers usually tend to suggest that the senate was a closed, largely hereditary body, to which access was difficult for those who did not belong to a limited number of aristocratic families. Some modern scholars have however advanced the view that in reality the senate was much more open to newcomers than the ideology of the Roman aristocracy would imply.

In essence, the debate revolves around the weight we should place on ancient literary texts which emphasise the exclusivity of the senate. Two passages, taken from Cicero and Sallust respectively, illustrate the problem.

Attacking L. Calpurnius Piso Caesonianus (who had been consul in 58 BC, the year in which Cicero had been exiled, and had also been responsible for looting marble columns from the ruins of his house), Cicero observed:

> You were made aedile: it was *a* Piso – not that man Piso there – that was chosen by the Roman people. In the same way, the praetorship was conferred on your ancestors – they were dead, but well known; you were alive, but no-one yet knew you. But when the Roman people elected me high among the quaestors, then first aedile, then first praetor, by the votes of all the centuries, it was to an individual man they bestowed the honour, not to my family; to my character, not to my ancestors; to my clear distinction rather than to any supposed nobility.
>
> (CICERO, *Against Piso* 2)

Likewise Sallust on C. Marius, a 'novus homo' and protagonist in the

political and military struggles of the late second and early first centuries
BC:

> He did not dare to seek the consulship; for even though the *plebs*
> conferred the other magistracies, the nobility passed the con-
> sulship to each other from hand to hand. There was no new man
> so eminent or so distinguished in his achievements that he was
> not considered unworthy of the honour and the consulship
> almost polluted by such a man holding it.
>
> (SALLUST, *Jugurtha* 63).

The point of Cicero's attack is that it was Piso's distinguished family that
was honoured by the voters rather than Piso the individual. Sallust
stresses the special difficulties experienced by 'new men' such as Marius
in gaining access to the consulship. Central to the issue here are the terms
nobilis ('noble' – literally 'well-known') and *novus homo* ('new man'),
which were commonly used in Roman political language. The general
sense is clear, but how far they have a precise meaning has been a subject
of debate. *Nobilis* is variously taken to mean 'a man with a consul or
consuls among his ancestors' or 'a man with magistrates (or patricians)
among his ancestors' (a rather weaker formulation); a *novus homo* could
be defined as 'a man without senatorial ancestors' who rises to enter the
senate or, alternatively, to become consul. The difficulty involved in
defining these terms and using them in an analysis of the political system
is that passages containing this language almost invariably derive from
political or lawcourt oratory or historical narratives, in which the writer
or speaker is keen to prove a point or put over a particular point of view.
Each definition has therefore to be treated with a certain degree of
caution.

A potentially more productive approach, which can usefully be combined with the analysis of the terminology used by ancient writers, is to
go back to the data for office-holding, derived from the Fasti – the official
list of Roman magistrates which was displayed by Augustus in the Forum
Romanum – together with information on magistrates derived from Livy
and other historical writers, and examine directly the patterns of office-
holding. It has been shown that despite the prevailing ideology of the
exclusivity of the senate, 35% of consuls in the period between 249 and
50 BC had no known direct consular ancestor in the previous three
generations, and 32% no known son who became a consul. Several
explanations can be provided, both financial and demographic. A political career was a high-risk venture and an extremely expensive one:

almost of necessity it involved an ostentatious lifestyle, and getting elected (as discussed in Chapter 5) also involved considerable expenditure. Those who were successfully elected could recoup this outlay by taking on the governorship of a province after their year of office. This could be highly lucrative if the governor conducted a successful military campaign or turned a blind eye to abuses by tax-collectors and others (or even participated himself); those who failed to be elected were left with massive debts and could even be expelled from the senate by the censors, bringing their political ambitions to an untimely end, whether or not they had distinguished ancestors.

A more general problem was that life expectancy in antiquity was short, hygiene was poor and medicine pre-scientific. In time of political strife or civil war, the members of the elite were in particular danger: 90 senators were killed in Sulla's proscriptions, 300 in those of the triumvirs in 43 BC. Early death must have robbed many families of sons whom they hoped would follow their fathers into the senate.

Both financial and demographic considerations must therefore have affected the reproductive strategies of wealthy families. If we assume that average life expectancy at birth for a member of the Roman aristocracy was 30 years (plausible for a pre-industrial society), infant mortality is likely to have been very high indeed. It has been estimated that of 1000 births only 744 children would survive to the age of one year and 589 to the age of ten; fewer than 392 would typically survive to the age of 42, the first year in which a consulship could be held, according to legislation of 180 BC. Aristocratic families therefore needed to produce many children in order for some of them – the males – to have a chance, having survived into adulthood, of successfully pursuing a political career. However, if many of the the children did in the event survive, the family would face a new problem: it was normal for an estate to be divided between surviving children, so each of them, male and female, would inherit a proportion, and it might be impossible for the male children successfully to pursue individual political careers with the resources that were left to them.

The impact of these trends would have been to ensure that there was a constant flow of members of families in and out of the senate, which was therefore much more open to new blood than many of the ancient texts have suggested. We should bear in mind, however, that it was as much in the interest of those who had entered the senate without distinguished ancestors as those who did have illustrious families to stress the exclusivity of that body, and therefore the impressiveness of their achievement in entering it.

Nevertheless, there does seem to have been a significant difference in patterns of access between the lower magistracies and the consulship, the most prestigious of the annual magistracies, where the proportion of 'new men' appears to have been significantly smaller than in the lower echelons of the senate. There also seems to have been a significant difference between the second century BC and the last twenty years of the Republic, when fewer still without consular ancestry gained the consulship. Sallust may have been close to the truth in stating that 'the nobility passed the consulship to each other from hand to hand'; Cicero less so in implying that his own achievement in being elected quaestor was very exceptional. No doubt the different composition and character of the *comitia centuriata* (which elected the consuls) and the apparently more 'democratic' *comitia tributa* (which elected the quaestors) lay in part behind the greater ease with which a 'new man' could gain the quaestorship. Another contributing factor was that there were (from Sulla's time) twenty vacancies available to would-be quaestors, but only two for aspiring consuls.

Current debates

Current scholarship on the politics of the Roman Republic is characterised by a series of energetically contested debates. In the past some scholars have stressed the hereditary nature of the Roman aristocracy, and, in parallel, suggested that the Roman political elite had close control over the rest of the population by means of closely defined networks of patronage. Others have emphasised instead the comparative openness of the oligarchy, looser forms of elite control over the masses, and a greater degree of popular participation. What is clear is that only wealthy individuals were able to take on political office, and thus able to take a leading role in public life as members of the senate. Individuals and their ambitions were of central importance to the way the political system worked, so it is essential to look in some detail at the competitive nature of the Roman aristocracy – and the ways in which it had an impact on the city of Rome and its population – before examining the different techniques used by political leaders to persuade voters to support them.

Chapter 4
Aristocratic competition in the city of Rome

The competitive aristocracy

The Roman aristocracy was an extremely competitive body both within the sphere of formal politics and beyond; in fact, it is difficult to identify any aspect of aristocratic life which was not bound up with politics in some way or another. Two anecdotes reported about Julius Caesar illustrate this neatly. Plutarch notes:

> It is said that, when Caesar was crossing the Alps and was passing by a miserable barbarian village inhabited only by a handful of people, and his friends jokingly wondered whether there were struggles for office, contests for pre-eminence, and rivalries of powerful men here too, Caesar said to them with a very serious expression that he would rather be first man here than second at Rome. (PLUTARCH, *Caesar* 11)

The second-century AD biographer Suetonius tells us that Caesar was frequently heard to say that:

> Now he was leading citizen, it would be harder to push him down from first to second place than from second to last place. (SUETONIUS, *Life of Caesar* 29)

This extreme form of competitiveness was not limited to Caesar himself and his contemporaries, whose rivalries were ultimately to bring down the Roman Republic; nor is it purely a product of the literary presentation of Caesar by Plutarch and Suetonius or their sources. The same concern to 'be the best' can be traced back to the mid Republic, in the tomb-monuments and funerary orations of the third century BC. The best known of these are probably the monumental sarcophagi enclosed in the Tomb of the Scipios, which was excavated in the eighteenth century on a road between the Via Appia and Via Latina, not far outside Rome's main southern gateway, the Porta Capena (see Fig. 1, p. 2).

The first (and most impressive) sarcophagus set up in the tomb is that

of Lucius Cornelius Scipio Barbatus, who held the consulship in 298 BC.
Barbatus' epitaph is as follows:

> Lucius Cornelius Scipio Barbatus, born from his father Gnaeus,
> a brave and wise man, whose appearance was as outstandingly
> excellent as his courage; he was consul, censor and aedile
> among you; he captured Taurasia and Cisauna, Samnium in
> fact; he subdued the whole of Lucania and took away hostages.
> *CORPUS OF LATIN INSCRIPTIONS (CIL)*, I² 6-7.

The dating of the sarcophagus itself and of the texts painted and inscribed
on it is controversial. It has been suggested by some scholars that the
inscribed text post-dates the death of Barbatus by many years, but others
have argued that the monument does indeed provide an authentic record
of the aristocratic ideology of the early third century BC, with its emphasis
on the deceased's exceptional personal bravery and appearance, as well
as his military achievements. Barbatus' son, also called Lucius Cornelius
Scipio, consul in 259 BC, was buried (perhaps not long afterwards) in the
same tomb, and his monument asserted that 'it is generally agreed that
this man was the very best of all good men at Rome' (*CIL* I² 9). This
phrase is almost identical to that which Cicero tells us was used on the
tomb of A. Atilius Calatinus, who was consul in 258 BC (the year after
L. Cornelius Scipio) and again in 254 BC: 'This one man most families
agree was chief man of his people' (CICERO, *On old age* 61). Two other
texts from the period of Rome's first war with Carthage similarly lay stress
on individual excellence: a monument set up in honour of C. Duilius,
who as consul in 260 BC defeated the Carthaginians in a sea-battle off
Milazzo on the north coast of Sicily, honoured him as the 'first man to
equip naval fleets...the first who granted the Roman people booty from
a sea-battle, and the first to lead free-born Carthaginians in triumph' (*CIL*
I² 25). The inscription was attached to a column decorated with ships'
prows set up in the Forum, and was re-carved in the mid-first century
AD, suggesting that it still maintained its significance some three hundred
years after the event. The funerary oration delivered by Q. Caecilius
Metellus in honour of his father L. Caecilius Metellus, consul in 251 and
247 BC, is preserved by Pliny the Elder. It described L. Metellus as the
first man to lead elephants in a triumph (they had been captured in a
Carthaginian attack on Palermo); he was said to have achieved the 'ten
greatest and best objects in pursuit of which wise men spend their lives':
to be a first-class warrior, an excellent orator, a valiant commander, to
have undertaken great operations and received the greatest honour, to be

exceptionally wise and considered the most distinguished senator, to have acquired great wealth in an honourable way, to leave behind him many children and to be the most eminent man in the state; 'and that these things had fallen to him, and to no-one else since the foundation of Rome' (PLINY, *Natural History* 7. 139-140).

Excelling in the state, and seeking to outdo all rivals, was therefore something towards which ambitious Romans of the ruling class typically set their aim. In fact the career and lifestyle of that class were largely defined by this competitiveness, which was also instrumental both in inspiring the expansion of Roman rule in Italy and overseas and in transforming the physical appearance of the city of Rome. Much of this competitive activity took place within the city and was played out before the populace of Rome.

Competition, military glory, triumphs and public building

Training in competitiveness began for the young Roman male at an early age. Polybius tells us that in his time the aspiring politician was obliged to serve for 10 years in the Roman army before being eligible for political office (POLYBIUS 6.19), and this seems to have been true at least up to the end of the second century BC; even afterwards many members of the Roman elite had substantial experience of military service. Achieving glory and prestige was central both to the political and the military life: Sallust, discussing the traditional virtues of the Roman Republic, commented that in past times:

> their greatest struggle for glory was with each other: each man endeavoured to strike the enemy, to scale a wall, and to be seen to do so. (SALLUST, *Catiline* 7)

It seems that even in the mid and late Republic it was not unknown for a Roman general to find himself pitted against an enemy commander in single combat, a situation in which individual excellence in fighting would obviously be crucial, and which would potentially contribute to an ideology of individualism. Commanders might adopt new names to commemorate great victories: P. Cornelius Scipio, who defeated Hannibal in 202 BC, took the *cognomen* Africanus, but in turn was outdone by his adoptive grandson P. Cornelius Scipio Aemilianus, who took two new names, Africanus and Numantinus, to commemorate victories over Carthage (in 146 BC) and at Numantia (in Spain, in 133 BC) respectively.

The culmination of a successful military expedition was the 'triumph', an honour granted by the senate only to those commanders who had defeated the enemy and killed at least 5000 of them in the process. The victorious army gathered in the Campus Martius, in the vicinity of the Villa Publica, and then on the day of the triumph itself formed into a procession which followed a traditionally prescribed route through the city. Senators and magistrates led the procession, with the spoils of war paraded through the city, together with placards and paintings to commemorate the achievements of the campaign. Then came the enemy captives and at the rear of the procession the commander himself, dressed in a red robe and with his face painted – perhaps to resemble the cult-statue of the god Jupiter – and accompanied in his four-horse chariot by a slave holding a crown over his head and repeating the words 'remember thou art mortal'. The soldiers themselves brought up the rear of the procession as it wound from the Campus Martius through the Circus Flaminius, entered the city by the Porta Triumphalis, crossed the Forum Boarium and moved along the Circus Maximus before skirting the Palatine, passing down the Via Sacra to the Forum Romanum, and then climbing up to the Capitoline hill where a sacrifice took place to Jupiter Optimus Maximus (Fig. 5).

The competitive instincts of the Roman aristocracy were manifested not only in the rivalry to achieve a triumph, but also, once this had been awarded, to make sure their triumph was an impressive and memorable one. The commemorative inscription of C. Duilius stresses his achievement in being the first Roman to distribute booty from a sea-battle and to lead free-born Carthaginians in triumph. Later *triumphatores* sought to outdo each other in novelty and originality, displaying ever more unusual captives, different types of booty, or employing innovations such as paintings of their campaigns: in 264 BC M. Valerius Maximus Messalla displayed a battle-scene from the First Punic War on the wall of the Curia. Triumphs expanded in length too, beyond the confines of a single day: the triumph of T. Quinctius over the Macedonians in 194 BC lasted three days, as did that commemorating L. Aemilius Paullus' victory over the Macedonians in 168 BC.

The triumph was intended as a celebration of military success, but integral to that celebration was the participation of the Roman people. Polybius refers to:

> the processions they [i.e. the Romans] call triumphs, in which
> the generals display their achievements clearly before the eyes
> of the citizens. (POLYBIUS 6.15.8)

The award of a triumph could be exploited for electoral advancement: Pliny the Elder tells us that in 146 BC L. Hostilius Mancinus displayed in the Forum a picture of his assault on Carthage and explained the details to passers-by, with such success that he was elected to the consulship for the following year (*Natural History* 35.23).

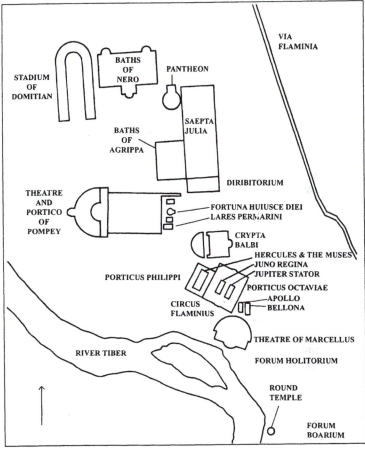

Fig 5 The Campus Martius in the early Empire.

The triumph as an institution had a more permanent effect on the appearance of the republican city, too. Generals frequently commemorated their victory and the triumph by spending some of the wealth acquired on campaign on public buildings for the city of Rome. Sometimes a temple might be vowed to the gods by the Roman general in the heat of battle, and then constructed as an expression of thanks when he returned successfully to Rome. Temples specifically said to have been set up *ex manubiis* ('from the booty') include those dedicated to Mars by D. Iunius Brutus in the late 130s following his campaigns in Spain, and that to Honos and Virtus ('Honour and Virtue') set up by C. Marius, after his victories over the Cimbri and Teutones, Gallic tribes who had invaded northern Italy at the very end of the second century BC. There may well have been others too.

During the third and second centuries BC, numerous temples were set up in the city either directly by the triumphal generals themselves or under the aegis of the senate. Of these a substantial proportion were located either on or close to the route of the triumphal procession, for example in the central part of the Campus Martius, in the Circus Flaminius (which by the late Republic was lined with temples on both sides), the Forum Holitorium and the Forum Boarium. These monuments not only represented the personal gratitude of the general – and the collective gratitude of the state – to the deities which had supported him and his army in the time of need, but can also be seen as contributing to the long-term prestige of the general's family. Several temples of this era have been investigated archaeologically, perhaps the best known being the four located in the middle of the Campus Martius and collectively known as the 'Largo Argentina temples' after the name of the modern square in which they are situated. Two of these are securely identified: one is the Temple of the Lares Permarini (the Lares of the Sea), which was vowed by L. Aemilius Regillus, who as *praetor navalis* in 190 BC was victorious in a sea battle against Antiochus of Syria (Fig. 6). It was dedicated by L. Aemilius Lepidus, censor in 179 BC, who set up a commemorative inscription, preserved for us by Livy:

> for bringing an end to a great war, for subjecting kings, this battle, undertaken for the purpose of establishing peace, gave victory to L. Aemilius, son of M. Aemilius... for this achievement he vowed a temple to the Lares of the Sea.   (LIVY 40.52)

Nearby was the Temple of Fortuna Huiusce Diei ('Fortune of this Day') which was vowed in 101 BC by Q. Lutatius Catulus at the battle of Campi Raudii against the Cimbri (Fig. 7, p. 36). (The two other temples are both dated archaeologically to the third century BC, but there is still some debate about the divinities to which they were dedicated.)

Aristocratic competitiveness might be reflected in either the location or the design of the temple. It is very striking that the Temple of Juno Regina – built in the Circus Flaminius (again overlooking the triumphal route) and dedicated by the same M. Aemilius Lepidus, who was censor in 179 BC – was located immediately adjacent to that of Hercules and the Muses, dedicated by M. Fulvius Nobilior, who also served as censor in 179 BC. Fulvius Nobilior and Aemilius Lepidus were notorious personal enemies, but when they were elected to serve as censors together the

Fig 6 The Temple of the Lares Permarini.

senate persuaded them to set aside their mutual antagonism. Similarly, in the mid-second century we see a series of temples constructed in increasingly exotic building materials, as marble of different kinds became available from areas newly conquered by Rome. We are told that the first temple in Rome built entirely of marble was that dedicated to Jupiter Stator in 146 BC by Q. Caecilius Metellus Macedonicus (it was located in the Circus Flaminius, and is not to be confused with the other temple dedicated to this deity on the slopes of the Palatine, where the senate met in 63 BC). The first surviving marble temple, however, is the round temple located in the Forum Boarium, suggesting that Caecilius Metellus set a new fashion in temple-building. An earlier attempt by Q. Fulvius Flaccus to build a temple to Fortuna Equestris with marble roof tiles (Livy says 'he devoted every effort to ensure that no temple at Rome should be larger or more magnificent' [42.3]) ended in failure when Flaccus was instructed to restore the tiles to the Temple of Juno Lacinia in the south Italian city of Croton from where he had misappropriated them.

In general, it appears that rivalry of this sort was more prevalent, and certainly more keenly expressed, as the second century BC wore on, presumably reflecting both increasingly severe political competition and increased resources for grandiose building projects. In this context it is striking that from the middle of the second century temples began to be

Fig 7 The Temple of Fortuna Huiusce Diei.

known by the name of their builders as well as that of the deity to which they had been dedicated – or even instead of it, suggesting an even greater focus on the individual temple builder. Caecilius Metellus' temple was known as the Aedes Metelli ('the shrine of Metellus'), Marius' Temple of Honos and Virtus was known as the Aedes Mariana, and Q. Lutatius Catulus' Temple of Fortuna Huiusce Diei as the Aedes Catuli, for example;

interestingly, the latter two temples had been vowed by different generals in the context of the same campaign against the Celtic invaders. In the last years of the Republic, however, the number of new temples being constructed appears to have fallen. Those few that are known, such as Pompey's Temple of Venus Victrix, or Julius Caesar's temple dedicated to Venus Genetrix, formed only one element in grandiose building complexes, such as the Portico and Theatre of Pompey on the Campus Martius, or the Forum of Caesar, which had the Temple of Venus as its centrepiece. There were by this time many alternative ways of spending money to gain prestige and advancement.

The construction of temples was, then, only one of the ways in which public building at Rome in the second and first centuries BC reflected the twin phenomena of overseas expansion and aristocratic competition. In the second century, new forms of monument began to be employed, including the *fornix* (arch): in 196 BC, L. Stertinius (who had not even requested a triumph) used the spoils of war to set up two arches in the Forum Boarium and another in the Circus Maximus, decorated with gilded statues. In 120 BC, the Fornix Fabianus was erected where the Via Sacra entered the Forum, to commemorate Q. Fabius Maximus' triumph over the Allobroges in that year.

Basilicas and porticoes, both monumental types which owed much to the colonnaded *stoa* of the Greek world, began to be constructed in Rome in increasing numbers: the porticoes were designed to provide an impressive monumental setting to surround temples and, like them, were often associated with the route of the triumph. The Porticus Octavia and Porticus Metelli, built by Cn. Octavius and Q. Caecilius Metellus Macedonicus following their triumphs in 168 BC and 146 BC respectively, were located in the Circus Flaminius. Nearby in the Campus Martius (and adjacent to the Temple of the Lares Permarini) was the Porticus Minucia, set up by M. Minucius Rufus to commemorate his victory as consul in 110 BC over the Scordisci. Basilicas (which had no religious associations: the association of the word with places of worship comes from the use of the basilica form by the early Christians for their churches) were constructed around the Forum from the early second century onwards: they provided a roofed space where the commercial, legal and political functions of the Forum could take place, safe from bad weather. These were normally built by the censors using public funds – for example, the Basilica Porcia by M. Porcius Cato in 184 BC, the Basilica on the north side of the Forum, constructed by M. Fulvius Nobilior in 179 BC but usually known as the Aemilia after a major rebuilding in the mid-first century, and the Basilica Sempronia by Ti. Sempronius Gracchus in 169 BC. The wealth used, as well as the architectural form, was derived indirectly from the conquest of the Greek East, even if they were less closely associated with a specific victory than the porticoes. Both porticoes and basilicas tended to take the name of their builder – whether triumphal general or censor – and the focus of appreciation was thus fully directed towards him, in a way that the identification of temples with their builders seems to have imitated.

Clearly the building operations of the second century BC had a major impact on the appearance of the city of Rome, but did the construction of a temple or a public monument have a significant effect on a politician's future career? In most cases, the answer must probably be 'no', because often these buildings were set up by those who had already achieved distinguished careers and had reached the consulship or the censorship. In any case, the games and feasts often provided as part of the triumphal celebrations were more likely to result in short-term prestige, as showing the generosity of the triumphal general. The benefit was probably felt more by the general's descendants, who would be able to point to the temple or monument as an indicator of their ancestor's distinction; and, often, to the *manubiae* (spoils of war) which were displayed in the temple. In Varro's account of how to rear birds (see Chapter 3), he describes the aviary at his estate near Casinum (modern Cassino), and compares its appearance with that of the Aedes Catuli (Temple of Fortuna Huiusce Diei) suggesting that this temple, together with its neighbours in the Largo Argentina group, was visible from the Villa Publica – and hence to the voters gathering there. The temples represented a permanent reminder of the achievements of Catulus, Aemilius Regillus and the other victorious generals. Similarly, from the second century BC onwards, political gatherings in the Forum took place in the shadow of the basilicas, which bore the names of distinguished families. The triumph was a celebration for senate and people alike, and the monuments set up in the aftermath of victories both commemorated the support of the gods for the Roman people and glorified the aristocratic families who took a leading role in those victories; but the distinction of these families was also commemorated in the city by other means, as we shall see.

Competition and the aristocratic house

After a triumph the victorious general was accompanied back to his home, the doorposts of which were decorated with spoils taken from the enemy. Pliny the Elder tells us that it was forbidden to remove spoils from the doorposts even when the property changed hands. A house which had belonged to an eminent general would therefore be instantly identifiable from outside, and the memory of his achievement would survive not only when the house was occupied by his descendants but even afterwards: 'the houses continued to celebrate a triumph even when their owners had changed' (*Natural History* 35.7). Some aristocratic houses destroyed in the Great Fire in Nero's reign still apparently had spoils attached to them. Unflattering comparisons were made between Pompey and Mark Antony, who occupied Pompey's house in the Carinae district after his death; the house had been decorated with prows from enemy ships captured by Pompey. The preservation of spoils in this way could on occasion be detrimental to public order: in 121 BC, the supporters of C. Gracchus seized weapons displayed in the house of Fulvius Flaccus (who had celebrated a triumph over the Gauls two years previously) and used them to take control of the Aventine hill.

The aristocratic house was closely identified with its owner and could potentially contribute to his public prestige in a very significant way. In an important passage Pliny the Elder contrasts the houses of the imperial period, decorated with Greek works of art, with those of the Republic:

> Things were different in the *atria* of our ancestors: there were not marble and bronze statues by foreign artists to be admired, but masks made out of wax were displayed in individual cupboards so that there might be images which could be employed in family funerals, and whenever a member of the household died the whole community of those who belonged to his family were there. Family trees were linked by lines to painted portraits; the archive rooms were filled with books and memorials of achievement in magisterial careers.
>
> (PLINY, *Natural History* 35. 6-7)

The *atrium* was the repository of the family's history. Anyone entering – and it was open to virtually all, since it was here that Roman aristocrats would receive their clients and political associates, and the daily ceremony of *salutatio* (see Chapter 5) took place – would see the masks, portraits and family trees which commemorated the great achievements of earlier members of the family. The importance of the displays is underlined by the efforts made by some to invent and embellish their family history if it appeared insufficiently distinguished. In the mid-second century BC, Cato the Elder made a speech urging that spoils should not be attached to houses unless they had been captured from the enemy, the implication being that unscrupulous individuals were buying weapons and then displaying them as if they had been captured in battle. Much later, Livy laments the difficulties caused for the historian by exaggerated and bogus family trees and documents:

> I think the tradition has been vitiated by eulogistic funerary orations and falsified inscriptions under portraits, each family seeking falsely to acquire for itself the glory of magistracies and famous deeds. (LIVY 8.40)

In addition to the body of historical material on display in the *atrium*, the design and decoration of the house also provided opportunities for the ambitious to outdo each other in ways less sanctioned by tradition than the display of spoils, paintings and archives. One of the most visible ways in which aristocratic competitiveness expressed itself was through ostentatious building – and decoration – of houses. It was a commonplace among ancient commentators that levels of luxury in housing had increased dramatically in the latter years of the Republic. Velleius, writing in the reign of the Emperor Tiberius, comments on the case of Aemilius Lepidus, the *augur*, who was rebuked by the censors of 125 BC for renting a property for 6000 sesterces: 'nowadays, if one pays so little for a house, one is hardly recognised as a senator' (VELLEIUS PATERCULUS 2. 10). Similarly, Pliny the Elder comments that:

> in the consulship of M. Lepidus and Q. Catulus (that is, in 78 BC) there was no finer house at Rome than that of Lepidus himself; but, by Hercules, only 35 years later the same house was not even in the hundredth place. (*Natural History* 36. 109)

Major recent excavations on the slopes of the Palatine, near the imperial Arch of Titus, have revealed the remains of an aristocratic house of the first century which is plausibly identified as being that of M. Aemilius Scaurus, aedile in 58 BC, famous as being one of the wealthiest of its day (Fig. 8).

Scaurus had built a lavish temporary theatre which was decorated with marble columns 38 feet high (it was customary for temporary theatres to be set up annually to provide a venue for the dramatic performances held as part of the regular *ludi* [games]). When Scaurus' theatre was demolished, he moved the columns into the massive *atrium* of his own house. The excavations revealed a small suite of baths and the remains of more than fifty small rooms for slaves in the basement of the house, giving a further indication of the scale and grandeur of the property.

Both the topographical investigation of the Palatine hill and examination of the literary sources for the first century BC demonstrate that Scaurus' house, although highly ostentatious, was not unique in its extravagance; during the latter years of the Republic, the area was densely inhabited by the Roman upper classes. Remains of houses of the second and first centuries BC have been discovered on the south-west

Fig 8 The slopes of the Palatine hill seen from above the Forum. The house of M. Aemilius Scaurus was located just in front of the Arch of Titus (in the rear of the photograph).

corner of the Palatine, overlooking the Circus Maximus, and beneath the later Flavian palace, as well as on the slope leading down from the hill to the Forum Romanum.

It is possible to reconstruct in some detail the ownership of houses in this area of the Palatine, and create a 'snapshot' of the neighbourhood on the basis of the rich literary sources available for the mid-first century BC. We know that Scaurus' house was an amalgamation of properties previously owned by his father and the adjacent house of the Octavius family. In 53 BC the house was purchased by Scaurus' next-door neighbour Publius Clodius, tribune in 58 BC and long-time enemy of Cicero, for the astronomically large sum of 14,800,000 sesterces. Clodius then combined the two properties together into a massive building. Next door to Clodius' house was that of Cicero (who had moved onto the Palatine in 62 BC, after the suppression of the Catilinarian conspiracy), and next door in turn to that was the house of Cicero's brother Quintus (who had moved there by 59 BC). It is very striking that the personal enmity between these individuals was, until Clodius' violent death in 52 BC at the hands of a gang of supporters of his rival T. Annius Milo, reflected in their housing arrangements, with Clodius and Cicero living literally next door to one another on the slopes of the Palatine. Rivalry over housing was thus an integral part of the long-term political rivalry of Clodius and Cicero; the family of Clodius, the aristocratic Claudii, had evidently occupied the slope of the Palatine for generations, so Clodius was able to sneer that Cicero 'had *bought* his house' (as opposed to having inherited it). Similarly, Pliny the Elder recounts an ill-tempered exchange between the censors of 92 BC, Cn. Domitius Ahenobarbus and L. Licinius Crassus (former owner of the site of Scaurus' house), over Crassus' luxurious urban property. This was well known for its exotic trees, six of which were still in existence when this area of the city was ravaged by the Great Fire of AD 64. 'Cnaeus Domitius, who was a man of impassioned nature and also inflamed with that sour sort of hatred which arises out of rivalry...' (*Natural History* 17. 3). As well as illustrating the extent to which the possession of houses was a focus for aristocratic competition, the episode is given particular edge by the recent identification of not only Crassus' house but also that of Ahenobarbus, on the upper part of the Via Sacra. The house of Ahenobarbus seems to have been on the hilltop subsequently occupied by the Temple of Venus and Rome, which means that the censors were, like Cicero and Clodius, close neighbours as well as rivals.

When Cicero was exiled in 58 BC for having had the Catilinarian conspirators executed without a formal trial in 63, it was decreed that his house be demolished; on his return the following year, it was restored at the expense of the state. Cicero's speech *De Domo Sua* ('On his house') expressed his outrage at being treated in the same way as various notorious 'enemies of the state' whose houses had been demolished in similar circumstances earlier in the history of the Republic. Sp. Cassius, Sp. Maelius and M. Manlius Capitolinus, all of whom had been accused of aiming at kingship, were punished not only by being put to death but by having their houses (and therefore their very memory within the state) utterly destroyed. A more recent precedent was the case of M. Fulvius Flaccus, consul of 125 BC, whose house was destroyed after he was killed fighting with Gaius Gracchus and his supporters only four years later; the Porticus Catuli was subsequently built on the site (which was located on the Via Sacra, the route of the triumphal procession) by Q. Lutatius Catulus, as another commemoration of his victory over the Cimbri. By contrast, when P. Valerius Publicola, one of the first consuls of the Roman Republic, realised he was being suspected of aiming at kingship because of the impressive size of his own house on the Velia (above the Forum), he was said secretly to have demolished the house himself in the middle of the night. Having too ostentatious a house was risky, but could reap political rewards. It was thought that Cn. Octavius, a previous occupier of the site of Scaurus' house who was a *novus homo*, secured some votes, and thereby gained the consulship in 165 BC, because of the impressiveness of his residence – though in reality his successful military career (he celebrated a triumph for his naval victory over the Macedonians and built the Porticus Octavia in the Circus Flaminius) must also, presumably, have played a significant part in his success.

Aristocratic rivalry, therefore, had a major impact on the appearance of the city not just in terms of the public buildings that were constructed by the competing aristocrats, but also by reason of the increasingly grand private houses which formed an important element in the urban landscape – especially on the Palatine and other areas around the Forum. The latter commemorated their present and past owners and their achievements to visitors and passers-by alike; they also acted as places of interaction between elite and people in a variety of ways which will be explored further in Chapter 5.

Aristocratic funerals & commemoration

The rivalry of Roman aristocrats continued even after their deaths. Funerary monuments like those of the Scipios recorded their achievements; Cicero and Livy, however, note that just as the commemorations in the aristocrat's *atrium* might be embellished to increase their prestige, so equally funerary inscriptions (or the funeral orations on which they may be assumed to have been based) might be altered to improve the achievements of the deceased. The case of Scipio Barbatus provides a clear illustration: the version of his victories recorded on the stone differs significantly from those preserved for us by Livy and by the triumphal Fasti, an Augustan document from the Forum which lists the grant of triumphs by the senate. It is therefore not easy for the historian to determine which, if any, of these accounts corresponds to the reality of events in 298 BC.

Tombs

Aristocratic tombs came to play an important part in the topography of the ancient city of Rome. Except in very abnormal circumstances, disposal of the dead was not allowed within the *pomerium*, the sacred boundary of the city; instead, burials or cremations took place outside the city and tombs tended in general to be located along the main roads leading out of the city. The tomb of the Scipios was on a road which lay between the Via Appia and Via Latina, not far outside Rome's Porta Capena; other tombs of noble families were located nearby. For example, excavations in 1956 revealed the remains of another tomb of the Cornelii, located 500 m. beyond that of the Scipios, on the other side of the Via Appia. This produced inscribed sarcophagi commemorating P. Cornelius Scapula (consul in 328 BC) and other members of his family, who are assumed to have owned estates here. Other aristocrats known to have been buried in the same area include the Metelli, the Servilii, and A. Atilius Calatinus (for whom see above, p. 30). Aristocratic tombs, though, were not confined to the Via Appia. The tomb of the Domitii (where the Emperor Nero was to be buried) was situated close to the Via Flaminia; the remains of a tomb recently found under the church of Santa Maria del Popolo have been identified with this monument. The discovery of a wall-painting depicting Roman and Samnite warriors in a tomb of mid-republican date on the Esquiline Hill has led some scholars to identify it as the tomb of Q. Fabius Maximus Rullianus, who held the consulship five times in the late fourth and early third centuries BC and won several major victories against the Samnites. It also gives us an idea of what the paintings publicly displayed during and after triumphs in this period might have looked like.

It appears that the earliest family tombs of this kind were underground chambers, with inscribed sarcophagi or wall-paintings enclosed within the tomb, and for the fourth or third centuries there is little indication of external monumental features to make them a major element in the urban landscape. In the second century BC, however, the increase in public building was paralleled by more overtly impressive tomb monuments. The Tomb of the Scipios acquired a monumental façade in the mid-second century BC, and just outside the Porta Capena the tomb of the Marcelli was decorated in the mid-second century with three statues and a boastful inscription honouring 'three Marcelli, nine times consul' (ASCONIUS 12C). In both these cases, there appear to be links between the family tombs and nearby temples: M. Claudius Marcellus, conqueror of Syracuse, had vowed a temple to Virtus, which, together with that of Honos, also stood just outside the Porta Capena and near the family tomb. The Temple of the Tempestates ('Storms'), assumed to be in the vicinity of the Via Appia, was vowed by L. Cornelius Scipio, consul in 259 BC (apparently when his fleet was caught in a storm off Corsica). Perhaps not long afterwards, he was himself buried in the Scipios' family tomb. The area outside the city walls of Rome, and in particular that along the Via Appia, the main road leading southwards from Rome, appears thus to have been an area of aristocratic competition in much the same way as the triumphal route in the Campus Martius or Circus Flaminius. It may be that these families owned land in this area; the tomb of Ser. Sulpicius Galba (probably the consul of 108 BC), discovered below the Aventine hill, was adjacent to the Horrea Galbana, warehouses belonging to Galba's family.

Monumental tombs such as those mentioned had an increasingly important impact on the urban landscape, and funeral commemoration and related rituals connected with the dead also provided an opportunity for further manifestations of aristocratic competition. Polybius gives a graphic account of the funeral of a Roman aristocrat; and representations on tombs and sculptural monuments also combine to contribute to our understanding of the rituals connected with the death of an aristocrat at Rome.

Funeral ceremonies

The cortège set out from the deceased's home (where the dead man was laid out in the *atrium*), accompanied by relatives and friends, and musicians playing horns and flutes. An important element in the procession consisted of actors or clients wearing the masks, normally kept in cupboards in the *atrium*, which depicted the deceased's famous ancestors. They were dressed in robes and carried insignia appropriate to the highest honour the ancestors had achieved during their lifetimes. The dead man would be carried to the Forum, where he would be propped up on the Rostra, the speakers' platform, and an address (like that of Q. Caecilius Metellus for his father discussed above, p. 30) would be delivered by his closest male relative, listing his achievements and those of his ancestors, before the procession set off for the burial or, more commonly, cremation at the family tomb. Polybius explains that the aim was to inspire young men to glorious deeds in emulation of the dead man and his family:

> From this constant renewal of the reputation of good men, the glory of those who perform great deeds is immortalised, and the fame of those who have done good for their country becomes well-known among the masses and handed down to future generations. But what is most important is that the young men are induced to endure all sufferings on behalf of the common welfare in order to achieve the glory that accompanies brave men. (POLYBIUS 6.54)

The orations were aimed at the Roman people, too:

> As a result it happens that the masses, not only those who were themselves involved in the achievements, but also those not present at the time, when they remember and see displayed what occurred, are affected with such feelings that the occurrence appears to be a loss for the whole state, not just those mourning the dead man. (POLYBIUS 6.53)

Cicero, however, drew attention to the way in which assertions of doubtful veracity were made in funeral orations, 'things which never happened, false triumphs, inflated numbers of consulships...' (*Brutus* 62), which consequently confused the historical record. Similarly, funerals were occasions on which imaginatively reconstructed genealogies could be presented, as for example when Julius Caesar claimed his aunt Julia was descended from both the Kings of Rome and the immortal gods.

The funeral ceremony was an overtly politicised event, symbolised by the address from the Rostra, which was normally used for *contiones* and meetings of the popular assembly in the Forum. After the interment there would be a funerary banquet, which might well be on a large scale and provided an opportunity for the dead man's family to involve the Roman populace in the commemoration still further. Livy records how the funeral ceremonies organised in 174 BC by T. Flamininus in honour of his late father lasted for four days, and included not only a banquet and a distribution of meat, but also a performance of *ludi scaenici* (stageshows) and a gladiatorial display lasting three days which involved 74 pairs of fighters. Gladiatorial combats had became increasingly important as a feature of the aristocratic funeral: the first recorded example was the funeral games organised by D. Junius Brutus in 264 BC for his father, when three pairs of gladiators fought to the death in the Forum Boarium. Thereafter there was significant inflation in the numbers of fighters involved. The funeral of M. Aemilius Lepidus in 216 BC involved 22 pairs of gladiators; that of M. Valerius Laevinus in 200 BC 25 pairs; and that of P. Licinius in 183 BC 60 pairs. Because of the absence of Livy's text for the period, we are poorly informed about developments in the latter part of the second century BC but, given the competitiveness apparent in other parts of civic life, it would be surprising if numbers did not increase. In 65 BC, when he was aedile, Julius Caesar held games in memory of his father, who had died 20 years before, at which it was promised that 320 pairs of gladiators would fight, all of them with silver swords. It appears that in the event the numbers participating were reduced because of new legal restrictions on the number of gladiators to be kept in the city. This type of posthumous commemoration allowed members of the elite to stage games when it suited them politically (rather than when a family member happened to die), and Caesar subsequently held posthumous games for his aunt and daughter in the same way. Often these combats took place in the Forum itself, where a temporary elliptical arena was laid out. From c. 70 BC to the time of Augustus (when a new paving was installed in the Forum and covered them up), there were underground passages which allowed gladiators participating in these spectacles to emerge dramatically from the centre of the Forum; and it was normal practice for temporary stands to be set up to allow those members of the populace who could afford the seats to view the spectacles. In 122, C. Gracchus caused consternation by removing these stands in order to allow the people to view the spectacles for free.

Just as funerary orations were quasi-political events, so the gladiatorial spectacles took place in the predominantly political setting of the Forum. They enabled the aristocracy to commemorate the death of one of their number in front of, and with the full participation of, the people, although we must assume that normally only the most affluent members of the plebs, and perhaps clients and those favoured by the deceased's family, would in practice have been able to view these spectacles. The gladiatorial and theatrical events laid on for the benefit of the people occupied an ambiguous position between public and private, organised by individuals and private citizens but also becoming part of the official record of the year's events (which is why the details have been preserved for us). The funeral ceremonies also allowed competitive provision of entertainment for the people, with increasing levels of expense paralleling the increasing cost of public and private building – though it is quite likely that the extent of the spectacles and number of participants were liable to exaggeration by interested parties, as with other aspects of aristocratic competitiveness. As Dio gloomily commented (when discussing the number of gladiators who fought at the celebrations held by Julius Caesar to inaugurate his new Forum and the Temple of Venus Genetrix):

> if anyone wished to write down the number of those involved, he would find it a great effort, and he would not easily be able to determine the truth, for all these matters are often exaggerated through boastfulness. (DIO 43.22)

Funerals drew attention to the distinction of the family's past members and this in itself might be seen as contributing to the future success of its politically active members. It was vital, therefore, that the celebration be carried off in a suitably dignified and generous way, and the participation of the people was an essential part of the process.

Luxury and sumptuary laws

Funerals – and the gladiatorial combats often associated with them – were ostensibly private acts of piety organised to commemorate a deceased relative; yet organising grand public events in the city was in any case an obligation of the aediles, who had the responsibility for running the several annual *ludi*, in honour of different gods, which would involve the staging of drama, chariot-racing and other entertainments. The permanent impact of these events on the urban landscape was limited, since plays might often take place on the steps leading up to the podia of temples like that of Magna Mater on the Palatine; and temporary theatre buildings only were permitted until the construction of the first permanent theatre by Pompey in 55 BC. The opportunity for generosity and ostentation offered by the construction of a temporary theatre was great (as the case of M. Aemilius Scaurus shows, see p. 40) and, paradoxically, the transient nature of the monument perhaps contributed still further to the sense of extravagance involved.

Reckless expenditure on the organising of public festivities could be condoned as being for the benefit of the Roman people, but extravagance in private life was something which caused serious concern to the Roman senate. As Cicero put it, 'the Roman people hate private luxury, but they love public magnificence' (*In support of Murena* 76). This appears to have been a particular area of worry in the second century BC, when the Roman conquest of the Greek East, and the gradual elimination of external enemies, coupled with the influx of wealth and booty on a hitherto unknown scale, not to mention unprecedented levels of exposure to Greek culture, led moralists to fear for the well-being of Roman society. Historians variously ascribed the beginning of Rome's moral decline to 186 BC (Livy), 168 BC (Polybius), 154 BC (Calpurnius Piso) or 146 BC (Sallust), and blamed this on the absence of serious foreign enemies or on the influx of wealth and luxury. That this was not purely a retrospective analysis devised by moralistic historians is suggested by the repeated initiatives on the part of the senate during the course of the second century BC to clamp down on luxury. The earliest known example of a sumptuary law is the restriction on funerary expenditure in the mid-fifth century BC Twelve Tables (itself perhaps derived from similar provisions in the sixth-century law-codes of the Athenian Solon), while the *Lex Oppia* of

215 BC, passed in the midst of Rome's war with Hannibal – restricting the wearing of multicoloured dresses by women and their ownership of gold – was revoked in 195 BC in the aftermath of the Roman victory, following mass protests by the women of Rome. Other pieces of legislation do, however, seem to fit in with the view expressed by Polybius that the defeat of Rome's foreign enemies and the influx of wealth resulting from this success allowed greater levels of expenditure than had previously been possible (31.25), and the fact that legislation is introduced at all is striking – previously such matters had been the responsibility of the censors.

Thus the *Lex Orchia* of 182 BC restricted numbers of dinner guests; an anecdote in Plutarch suggests that the law was being so vigorously enforced by the censor of 169 BC that citizens extinguished their lights as he passed by for fear of detection (*Tiberius Gracchus* 14). The *Lex Fannia* of 161 BC restricted expenditure on dinners on festive days to 100 asses (10 asses only on normal days) plus vegetables, bread and wine, and established that a maximum of 100 lbs of tableware was to be used at dinner (another instance of inflation of extravagance: in 275 BC P. Cornelius Rufinus had been expelled from the senate for possessing just 10 lbs of silver tableware). The *Lex Didia* of 143 BC reinforced the provisions of the *Lex Fannia*, extended them to Roman citizens living in Italy and enacted that the guests – as well as the host – of a banquet not conforming with the law should be punished. Two further pieces of legislation, the *Lex Licinia* (probably of the late second or early first century BC) and Sulla's *Lex Cornelia* of 81 BC (increasing the maximum expenditure allowable on festive days to 300 asses) are also known.

Various explanations are possible for the introduction of sumptuary laws, and for the concerns expressed by the senate about luxurious eating in particular. Worries about the moral consequences of luxury must have been one consideration behind these initiatives, but the chief motivating factor behind the laws seems to have been a concern within the senate about individuals using their wealth to advance their own cause to the detriment of that body as a whole – lavish entertainment was seen as a means of buying influence. The implication is that the increasing availability of wealth from new sources was increasing tensions both within the senate and with the affluent outside that body. Individuals were coming to have an influence which was regarded as excessive, and upward social mobility brought about by new sources of wealth was also a cause of worry. As Polybius put it:

it is clear that as prosperity becomes established in the state, lifestyles will become more extravagant, and the men of the state more competitive about public office and everything else than they ought to be. (6.57)

Aristotle had argued in the fourth century BC that aristocracies tend to collapse either through the extravagance of their members, the creation of a second, narrower, aristocracy within its ranks, or an appeal to democracy and degeneration into mob rule. All of these tendencies the senate would be seeking to avoid.

Other laws passed in the same period, including several against *ambitus* (bribery: see Chapter 5 for a discussion), together with restrictions on expenditure at games, collectively tend to confirm this impression of senatorial concern to maintain the solidarity of the senate in the face of increasing individualism. One area where new legislation seems to have been related to these concerns was the repeated tenure of public office.

Repeated tenure of public office

Although it is most apparent in the second century BC, this concern about individual senators coming to have excessive influence within the collectivity that was the senate seems to have a long history. From the time that it began to become a permanent body rather than a temporary council of advisers, attempts were made to curtail excessive influence on the part of individuals, in particular by laying out a sequence in which magistracies had to be held, and placing restrictions on the repeated holding of consulships by individual members of the senate. The *Lex Genucia* of 342 BC banned the holding of a magistracy more than once within ten years, and analysis of the record of consulships preserved in the Fasti seems to suggest that this was indeed put into effect until difficult circumstances in the Second Samnite War of the late fourth century BC led the Romans to re-elect able generals such as L. Papirius Cursor and Q. Fabius Maximus Rullianus to repeated consulships (both of them served as consul no fewer than five times in their career). The rule seems to have been re-implemented from 290 BC until 216 BC, when, following the disastrous defeats at Trasimene and Cannae, the restrictions were again slackened to allow leaders with proven military experience, such as M. Claudius Marcellus, to hold office repeatedly. At the end of that conflict, however, the *cursus honorum* (sequence of offices) was again enforced, and was backed up by the *Lex Villia Annalis* of 180 BC. This reiterated the principle of a ten-year interval between offices, and laid down minimum ages for each office: 25-30 for the quaestorship, 36 for the aedileship, 39 for the praetorship and 42 for the consulship. With the exception of Scipio Aemilianus (who was consul in 147 and 134 BC) and C. Marius (who held the consulship on six occasions in the years after 107 BC, at the time of the invasion of Italy by the Germanic Cimbri and Teutones), no members of the senate held a repeated consulship at all between 152 BC and the dictatorship of Sulla (82 BC), who himself made a point of reinforcing the *Lex Villia Annalis* – again to consolidate the authority of the senate.

The difficulty the senate faced was that it had to strike a balance between on the one hand allowing successful and ambitious individuals to monopolise offices such as the consulship – and thus gain power and influence beyond that of their contemporaries – and on the other allowing a situation in which the security of the state would be endangered by being in the hands of comparatively inexperienced and perhaps incompetent commanders. It largely succeeded in this aim in the second century but at the cost of several disastrous military setbacks, most notably in Spain, with corresponding losses in terms of human life and declining income for the state. Typically, Roman military failures in the second century were blamed on a lack of support from the gods or lack of commitment on the part of the soldiers, but rarely on the generals in command. However, in time of real crisis – for example the attack on Italy by the Cimbri and Teutones – there were likely to be strong arguments (and popular pressure) for a successful general like Marius to be re-appointed to the command.

Moreover, despite the efforts of the senate, the pressure of competition in the Roman state continued to increase still further. The difficulty was a long-term one: as Rome's overseas dominions expanded and the city of Rome itself began to grow substantially, the senate responded, as we have seen, by increasing the number of quaestorships and praetorships. This improved opportunities for those who sought entry to the senate or advancement within it, but there were still only two consulships, and the consequence was that the rivalry between those seeking high office became more and more heated.

Conclusion

Aristocratic competition was a major feature of virtually all aspects of life in republican Rome and this had paradoxical consequences. On the one hand, competition was a force which impelled aristocrats to achieve glory and prestige and was instrumental in expanding Rome's empire, and, as such, contributed significantly to the expansion of Roman power. At the same time, excessive competition within the elite was potentially damaging to the collective authority of the senate, which took measures to curtail the repeated holding of office and excessive and ostentatious extravagance. Competition had a major impact on the appearance of the city, as rival politicians sought to commemorate their family's achievements with tomb monuments and public buildings, and to outdo their rivals in the luxury and extravagance of their lifestyles. Although the competitive ideology itself can be traced back to the earlier years of the Republic, there are indications that the level of competition increased significantly through the second and first centuries BC, as overseas conquests and more intensive agricultural practices meant that more disposable wealth became available for the elite. That wealth was manifested in increasing levels of expenditure on housing, more elaborate funerary commemoration (on gladiatorial games, in particular) and public building, and increased employment of slaves both on rural estates and in urban households. At the same time the increasing numbers of junior magistracies meant that achieving the highest eminence in the state by holding the consulship became much more difficult.

What is perhaps most striking is that this competition took place before an audience. The quest for glory required an admiring public, and as fellow aristocrats were perceived as rivals as much as peers, competitive acts of ostentation also took place in the view of, or with the participation of, the Roman people – or at least certain elements within the Roman people. Triumphs and funerals took place in the public spaces of the city with crowds looking on, and public buildings forming a backdrop to them. The *atrium* of the aristocratic house was open to all, tombs were visible to passers-by, games and theatrical shows were open to those able to obtain a seat. Just as the Roman people were engaged in resolving the rivalries of the elite in the electoral assemblies, they were also witnesses of and participants in these less obviously political manifestations of aristocratic rivalry.

Chapter 5
The practice of politics

Aristocrats were the protagonists in political life and the intense competition which characterised politics spilled over into virtually all other aspects of their lifestyle; but the Roman people – or some of them – were the participants in the assemblies which listened to politicians' speeches, voted on their proposals, and elected them into office. Politicians were keen to persuade the electorate by a variety of means that varied from the honourable, to the dubious, to the downright illegal; and this chapter explores the different types of approach available to them.

A guide to electioneering

A central text for the practicalities of political life in the first century BC is the so-called *Commentariolum Petitionis*. This purports to be a letter from Cicero's brother Quintus, advising the orator how to plan his campaign for the election held in 64 BC for consular office the following year. Views differ as to the authenticity of the document, especially since it contains numerous echoes of Cicero's own election speech in *toga candida* (those standing for election wore specially whitened togas, hence our term 'candidate' from the Latin *candidus*, 'shining'). The implication is either that Cicero took Quintus' suggestions very literally and incorporated them into his speech (which seems implausible: it is unlikely that Cicero would both have taken up suggestions from his younger and less politically experienced brother, and then allowed this to be known), or that the *Commentariolum* was composed after the event, drawing on Cicero's actual election speech and other pieces of oratory. It may be that the work was composed as a rhetorical exercise to parallel the letter sent by Cicero to Quintus advising him on how best to govern a province. Yet the author seems exceptionally well informed about political conditions in the first century BC, and whatever view is taken of the authenticity of its supposed authorship, the text can be seen to provide valuable insights into the practical aspects of canvassing and organising a political campaign – with particular reference to the difficulties facing a *novus homo* without senatorial ancestors (as Cicero himself was).

The *Commentariolum* begins by advising the prospective candidate to repeat, almost daily, the phrases 'I am a new man, I seek the consulship, this is Rome' (*Comm. Pet.* 2), and stresses the different ways in which voters can be persuaded to support him. Oratory is of major importance, and is seen as a means by which the 'new man' can make up for the disadvantages of his status. Friends should be reckoned up and reminded that this election is the opportunity for repaying past favours; members of the nobility should be cultivated. 'Canvassing for magistracies', the author observes, 'can be categorised as assiduous pursuit of two aims, one concerned with the support of friends, the other with the will of the people' (*Comm. Pet.* 16).

Friends, broadly defined as 'anybody who displays goodwill towards you, cultivates you, or visits your house regularly' (*Comm. Pet.* 16) must be persuaded to support the candidate: members of his family circle, neighbours, clients and freedmen and even slaves (in case damaging gossip emanate from disgruntled slaves in the household); but also important men in general, the magistrates, and those influential in the voting centuries or tribes. The gathering of support in the various units of the voting assemblies is of particular importance, especially from senators, *equites*, and influential men from all ranks, including freedmen active in the Forum:

> Reckon up the whole city – all the *collegia* (popular associa-
> tions), *pagi* (rural districts) and the surrounding areas; if you
> make their leading men your friends, you will easily control the
> multitudes which remain.　　　　　　　　　　(*Comm. Pet.* 30)

This awareness of the way in which the divisions of the *comitia tributa* and *comitia centuriata* operate is reflected in the instruction to:

> make sure that you keep in your mind the whole of Italy set out
> according to its tribal divisions and take care that there is no
> town, colony, community or indeed any place in Italy in which
> you do not have sufficient support.　　　　　(*Comm. Pet.* 30)

The candidate should make a particular point of remembering carefully the names of possible rural supporters. The *equites*, too, are to be parti-cularly cultivated, with a view to gaining the support of their eighteen centuries.

The author of the *Commentariolum* devotes particular attention to those attending on the candidate, who are subdivided carefully into *salutatores* (those that call at the candidate's house), *deductores* (those who accompany the candidate when leaving his house for the Forum) and *adsectatores* (those accompanying the candidate in general). The *salutatores* often attend several houses on the same day, so it is essential for the candidate to show how much he particularly appreciates their visiting him in order to make sure that they support him when voting day comes. The *deductores* and *adsectatores* tend to be more committed to the candidate as an individual, and the candidate must show his particular gratitude to them, so that he is always surrounded by a substantial crowd when he walks to the Forum.

The concluding sections of the *Commentariolum* are concerned with efforts to gain the support of the Roman People as a whole: key elements here are the need to remember names, to be genial in dealings with possible supporters, to canvass continually, to demonstrate generosity in entertaining and doing favours. Reputation is also important, manifested by the support of tax-collectors, *equites* and members of the nobility alike, as well as large numbers of other supporters. At the end, the treatise deals with the problem of bribery, which is said to be widespread. While not recommending the practice to Cicero, it suggests instead that he engage his supporters to keep an eye open for signs of bribery, in the hope that the perpetrators will fear that Cicero is intending to have them prosecuted after the elections, and (interestingly) concludes by taking comfort from the fact that centuries may still vote for their preferred candidate regardless of bribery.

The *Commentariolum* thus provides a fascinating account of the more 'respectable' political techniques used in the mid-first century BC, and hints at the darker world beyond. Canvassing and entertainment are respectable, bribery and (still less) violence not so; but all four played an important part in the day-to-day life of politics, with the city of Rome as the physical setting.

Canvassing

The *Commentariolum* makes it clear that canvassing voters in public places was regular and normal practice for Roman politicians, and this is confirmed by a variety of other ancient texts. Elections on the Campus Martius themselves seem to have been considered good opportunities for canvassing by candidates for the following year, as those interested in the outcome waited for the result. Polybius comments on the behaviour of the young Scipio Aemilianus, who, unlike his aristocratic contemporaries 'devoting their energies to legal cases and greetings, spending their time in the Forum, and attempting to make themselves popular with the people in this way' (31.29), spent his time hunting instead. Roman practice was even imitated by Antiochus IV Epiphanes of Syria, who:

> would often remove his royal dress, put on a toga, and make a circuit of the marketplace like a candidate for election, shaking hands with some and embracing others, asking them to vote for him. (POLYBIUS 26.1)

Occasionally efforts to win popularity in this way were counter-productive: Valerius Maximus (an early first-century AD author of anecdotal handbooks) preserves the story of P. Cornelius Scipio Nasica, who, seeking to drum up support for his candidature as curule aedile, was 'shaking hands rather persistently, as candidates do', and jokingly asked one peasant if his hand was rough because he walked on it. The peasant and his friends took offence at Nasica's 'offensive superciliousness', word spread among the rural tribes, and Nasica lost the election (VALERIUS MAXIMUS 7.5.2). Politicians had to be seen to be seeking the support of the people, and this could not be relied on without a certain amount of effort on their part. Publicity of all kinds was valuable to a candidate: we have already observed how having an impressive house, or energetically recounting one's military achievements to passers-by, would have the effect of raising one's profile in a way which might reap benefits at election time. As Tacitus comments, apparently describing the Augustan period, 'the more handsome a man's wealth, house and apparel, the more his name and *clientela* became eminent' (*Annals* 3. 55).

The form an electoral campaign took might well vary significantly according to the candidate's background; one of the particularly interesting features of the *Commentariolum* is the light it casts on the strategy to be adopted by a *novus homo*. *Nobiles* would have been able to draw attention to their family's already high public profile – the long rows of masks displayed in the *atrium* of their house, or at the funeral of a family member, the family tomb on the outskirts of the city, temples and porticoes built by their ancestors after famous victories in the past, and the prestige the family name had acquired over generations. Historians loyal to the great families would record (and exaggerate) their achievements for posterity; from the 130s onwards we see coin-legends being used to commemorate the ancestors of aspiring politicians. *Novi homines*, by contrast, had to stress their own individual achievements or abilities: oratorical skills, for example (which allowed them also to gain favour by defending influential people in court), or military successes. Cicero – speaking in support of a client whose earlier achievements were largely in the military sphere, and himself an accomplished orator, so in both cases hardly an impartial source – argued that:

> those who excel in military glory have the greatest dignity... [and that]...often even men who were not nobles have achieved the consulship because of their expertise [in oratory] largely because this skill results in great goodwill, firm friendships and very substantial support. (*In support of Murena* 24)

Especially where they originated from outside Rome, *novi homines* often tended to stress the supposed traditional virtue of their upbringing by contrast with the laziness and decadence of the *nobiles*, aiming to model themselves either on heroes of early Roman history or on more recently successful *novi homines*, such as Gaius Marius, whose fiery rhetoric on this subject was notorious:

> the rash speeches, filled with arrogance and contempt, annoyed the nobles, as he cried out that he had taken the consulship as spoil from the softness of the well-born and wealthy, and he could boast before the people of his own wounds, not the memorials of the dead or the masks of other men.
> (PLUTARCH, *Marius* 9).

The *novi homines* from Italy should have been well placed – especially in the years after the Social War, when the Italians were granted the Roman citizenship – to exploit the political opportunities offered by the irregular distribution of the inhabitants of Italian towns in the voting tribes at Rome in the way recommended by the *Commentariolum*. In support of their candidature, they could often bring supporters to Rome from several towns close to their own, who would frequently be registered in different voting tribes. Cicero, speaking in support of Cn. Plancius, who was accused of beating his rival M. Juventius Laterensis in the aedileship elections of 55 BC by means of bribery, argues that Plancius had instead been able to defeat his *nobilis* opponent because of the loyalty and commitment of his supporters, who lived in several different communities near Plancius' home town of Atina and had travelled to Rome to vote for him. The *nobiles* had their own networks in Italy, too, which may account in part for the limited successes of the *novi homines* overall.

Patronage

In recent years there has been considerable debate about the importance of patron-client relationships in the politics of the later Roman Republic. Patronage is a familiar feature of depictions of Roman life in the imperial period, in authors such as Juvenal and Martial, and is represented as a long-term personal relationship between more and less well-off individuals. Clients are depicted regularly attending their patron's house and receiving gifts and (often meagre) dinners in return, together with other benefits of the patron's support, such as legal advice and the hope and expectation of assistance in the event of unforeseen disasters.

Certainly this form of social relationship was familiar in the republican period too. In fact, the Roman aristocratic house, with its focus on the *atrium*, was designed so that clients and other associates of the owner could be received in a semi-public open space at the centre of the property. It was here that the family trees, masks and other relics documenting the family's achievements were displayed. Roman politicians had no office or other 'place of work' outside their own houses, which meant that much of their political activity had to take place in their own home. As Cicero puts it:

> in the house of an eminent man, in which numerous guests must
> be entertained and a multitude of every kind of people received,
> care must be taken to make it spacious.
>
> (CICERO, *On Duties* 1. 139)

The choice of houses by politicians was partly determined by their location and partly by their suitability for receiving large groups of clients: Cicero moved to a house on the Palatine, we are told, in order to save his clients a long walk (PLUTARCH *Cicero* 8); while C. Gracchus moved from the Palatine to a house in the vicinity of the Forum. This was perceived as 'more democratic' since the region around the Forum was where the poorer citizens tended to live. The *Commentariolum* similarly suggests that this type of relationship was of considerable significance in the contact between rich and poor. The practice of attending on the patron, whether as *salutator*, *deductor*, or *adsectator*, was commonplace and greeting him at his house in the morning, accompanying him to the Forum, or following him around all day in order to impress passers-by with the extent of his support, were all ways in which the less affluent could demonstrate their respect for and loyalty to a patron, at the cost only of their own time. Patronage was perceived as one of the central features of Roman society, and the importance and antiquity ascribed to the institution is shown by the fact that it was believed by Dionysius of Halicarnassus to have been created by Romulus, Rome's first king. The importance of patronage-relationships in Roman society is evident but what is less clear is how *politically* important patronage was. Since there are few overt references to patronage in contemporary accounts of the politics of the late Republic, it is likely that, although the elite used the obligations of patronage to induce their social inferiors to vote for them, it was just one technique among many rather than being of unique importance. The question remains whether the importance of patronage in political life – in relation to other means of persuasion – became more or less significant in the latter years of the Republic.

One way of approaching the problem may be to stress the diversity of situation in both geographical and chronological terms. Patronage, it might be argued, is more likely to be an effective means for an elite to control the masses in a comparatively small, and preferably rural, community, with little scope for social mobility – especially where ties of patronage are reinforced by tenancy agreements, or practical reliance on the major landowner in time of crop-failures or financial difficulties of some other kind. By contrast the inhabitants of a large city, with a high level of immigration and emigration (as was the case with Rome in the late Republic), might be thought to be substantially less likely to be tied into a long-term relationship with a particular individual or family, except where special circumstances existed: for example where the client was an ex-slave of the patron (freedmen were expected to show particular support and deference to their former masters) or where the client was resident in a property owned by the patron. The growth of the city in the second century BC and still more in the first century, and as a result the decreasing extent to which Rome was a 'face-to-face society', would (we might imagine) mean that patronage became less important in the later years of the Republic. The increasing independence of popular politicians – following the lead of tribunes like Ti. and C. Gracchus – played a role in contributing to this general trend, together with the introduction of the secret ballot in the 130s BC. Interestingly, Dionysius blames C. Gracchus for the breakdown in good relations between upper and lower classes which in his view led to the Civil Wars, so he evidently regards the decline of deference as a trend associated with the latter years of the second century BC. This must presumably have been accentuated as the Roman state, under the influence of radical tribunes, increasingly began to take upon itself the type of activity that had previously been considered the responsibility of patrons: for instance by providing low-cost – or eventually free – grain for some of the citizens of Rome. The incidence of debt as a problem in the first century BC, and in particular in the late 60s BC (when moneylenders sought to call in loans to invest in more lucrative markets after Pompey's successful reorganisation of the provinces of Asia Minor) might also be related to a decline in the influence of patronage-style relationships between the rich and the less well off.

Another possible way of understanding the role of patronage in politics is to investigate more closely how it related to the hierarchies within Roman society below the political elite. The formally hierarchised structure of the *comitia centuriata* shows that Roman society below the elite was not conceived as an undifferentiated mass of the 'poor'; rather there was a keen awareness of difference in status below elite level. Tacitus, discussing the reaction in Rome to the death of Nero, draws a distinction between the 'respectable part of the plebs, and those linked to the great houses', who were pleased and relieved at Nero's demise, and the 'filthy plebs, devoted to the circus and theatre', who lamented his death (*Histories* 1.4). The implication of Tacitus' analysis is that those most closely attached to the great houses – and understood as being most involved in relationships of patronage – are to be distinguished from the mass of the plebs. The poorest citizens were least able to provide useful electoral assistance for the patrons, as they occupied the lowest classes in the *comitia centuriata* and would need to seek help from wherever it was available. The more affluent clients, on the other hand, would have been reluctant to be described as such, preferring instead to be thought of as *amici* (friends): 'those who consider themselves wealthy... think it is as bad as death to make use of a patron or be called clients' (CICERO, *On Duties* 2.69). This in itself may help to explain the relative invisibility of patronage in republican politics, given the centrality of the institution within Roman society; and in any case it is also likely that individual loyalties were strained within the context of fiercely fought political competition, especially where an individual client had ties of obligation to more than one of the contestants in an election.

Bribery

The poet Lucan, writing in the mid-first century AD, blamed bribery and violence as two key elements in the fall of the Roman Republic, and these phenomena also are indicators, arguably, of the breakdown of traditional patronage structures.

Might was the measure of right: from this came laws and
popular decrees passed by force, disruption to the law caused
by tribunes and consuls; public office was seized by bribery,
and the people sold its own favours; corruption, lethal to the
city, repeated the annual struggles in the venal Campus.

(LUCAN, *Civil War* 1. 175-180)

Both of these means of 'persuading' the voters were of course illegal –
laws against *ambitus* (distinguished from the more respectable *ambitio*,
'ambition', and meaning literally 'going-round' the electorate) were
frequently passed during the second and first centuries BC. The *Lex
Cornelia Baebia de ambitu* was passed in 181 BC, and other pieces of
legislation followed: in 159 BC, under Sulla, in 67 BC (the *Lex Calpurnia
de ambitu*) and then in 63 BC during the consulship of Cicero. It is striking
that the *Lex Cornelia Baebia* was passed a year after the sumptuary *Lex
Orchia* of 182 BC and the year before the *Lex Villia annalis* of 180 BC,
which restricted the repeated tenure of magistracies (see Chapter 4). The
fact that these three pieces of legislation, all concerned with the danger
of ambitious and unscrupulous individuals gaining unfair advantage over
their senatorial fellows, were passed within three years of each other is
presumably not coincidental, and must be due to increasing levels of
competition at that time. In 180 BC the number of praetorships was
temporarily reduced from 6 to 4, apparently to reduce the level of rivalry
for the consulship, while Livy tells us that in the censorship elections of
189 M'. Acilius Glabrio, a *novus homo*, had come under suspicion because of his popularity with the masses. This was thought to have been
a result of his generosity with his wealth, and he had to withdraw his
candidature after it was alleged he had misappropriated booty captured
from King Antiochus of Syria the previous year (LIVY 37.57). Allegations of bribery become especially frequent in the last twenty years of
the Republic, as the laws were repeatedly broken and the lawcourts
became a political battleground; many of the legal cases about which we
are informed in this period (from Cicero's letters and speeches, in
particular) are concerned with allegations of this sort. The *Commentariolum* recommends that the candidate's associates keep a close eye on the
opposition and their supporters, in case bribery is detected and a prose-
cution needs to be undertaken.

One of the main difficulties in understanding the role of bribery in
republican politics is that there was a very fine dividing line between
corruption of the people (which was deplorable) and entertainment of
clients, friends and fellow-members of one's voting-tribe (which was

admirable), although laws became increasingly restrictive of practices on the borderlines. The evidence of the *Commentariolum* is complemented by that deriving from Cicero's speech in support of L. Licinius Murena, who was prosecuted for bribery at the consular elections of 63 BC for office to be held the following year. Cicero sought to defend him by arguing that his electoral campaign had consisted of entertainment which conformed with tradition, and had not been illegal.

Entertaining fellow members of one's tribe seems to have been considered respectable enough. The *Commentariolum* recommends that the candidate show his generosity by organising banquets for the people, either directly or through friends. In fact, it was essential if the candidate was to achieve popularity. Cicero tells the cautionary tale of Q. Aelius Tubero, a follower of the Stoic philosophy, who provided goatskins and coarseware cups (rather than luxurious coverings and vessels of precious metal) for the funerary banquet of Scipio Aemilianus, and failed to be elected praetor as a result (*In support of Murena* 75). Another possibility was to provide free seats for voters at gladiatorial games: Cicero's law of 63 BC prohibited a candidate from holding games in the two years before taking office, in order to avoid abuse of this type of generosity. Together with manifestations of generosity of this type went more flagrant instances of bribery. There was a quasi-formal structure of bribery agents, known as *divisores*, who organised the distribution of cash to voters in the tribes and centuries. Naturally this business was discreetly conducted but it seems that they had their headquarters in the area of the Circus Flaminius, not far from the voting-enclosure on the Campus Martius.

How did the practice of bribery work? The different structures of the *comitia centuriata* and *comitia tributa* meant that bribery would need to be deployed in different ways in each assembly. In the *comitia tributa*, money would have been distributed, via the *divisores*, indiscriminately to members of a particular tribe. It was in the *comitia centuriata*, however, where bribery seems to have been a particular problem, presumably because it was here that the most senior magistrates – censors, consuls and praetors – were elected, and it was possible to target particular groups of voters according to their place in the hierarchy. Arguably the citizens in the lower voting classes might have been more open than their wealthier counterparts to financial inducements to vote for one candidate rather than another; but the degree of affluence required to be a member even of Class I might (on some interpretations of the property qualification involved) not have been very substantial. In any case, the more competitive the elections were, and the more candidates that stood, the more likely that the lower centuries would be called on to vote and perhaps play a decisive role. In the consulship elections for the year 63 BC, for example, Cicero was elected first 'by the consensus of all' but the second consul elected, C. Antonius Hybrida, defeated his nearest rival, Catiline, by a margin of a few centuries 'since on account of his father's reputation he had a slightly more respectable body of supporters than Catiline did' (ASCONIUS 94C). In this sort of situation, a modest investment in bribing the lower centuries might well have brought worthwhile returns and made the difference between success and failure. An alternative strategy was that tried in the consular elections for 53 BC, where a substantial bribe was offered to the *centuria praerogativa*, the century selected by lot to declare its vote first, which was thought to have a disproportionate influence on the overall result. Whereas entertainment was seen as a normal element in patronage relationships, bribery was frowned on but, like patronage, it represented just one of a spectrum of electoral techniques which might be used to gain office. If failure to be elected was going to result in financial ruin for a particular senator (in which case he would be expelled from the senate anyway), the temptation to employ illegal means to secure election must have been very great. The impact on standards in political life was likely to be significant, though, as a vicious circle developed; the cost to individuals of keeping up with the increasing level of corruption in public life contributed significantly to the expenditure involved in a political career, which then was most likely to be recouped, in the event of success, from the hapless citizens of the province in which the successful politician was subsequently installed as governor.

Violence

Violence was an increasingly common feature of political life from the late second century BC onwards. Yet there had always been a tradition of 'self-help' at Rome as far as implementation of the law was concerned, and the stories that surrounded the expulsion of the kings and the killing of those (like Sp. Maelius) who allegedly aimed at kingship, provided a historical model for the use of force in the political sphere. A hint of what was to come is given by an episode in 185 BC when, according to Livy, *vis Claudiana* ('Claudian force') was (successfully) employed by Ap. Claudius Pulcher in order to have his brother elected consul (39.32.12-13). The 180s have already been seen to be a period of particularly vigorous political rivalry, and presumably what is implied by *vis Claudiana* is the intervention of clients and supporters of the Claudii in support of their candidate, to intimidate the electorate.

Violent incidents occurred during the tribunates of Ti. and C. Gracchus: both brothers met their deaths in clashes with senatorial traditionalists and their supporters, as did another radical tribune, L. Appuleius Saturninus, in 100 BC. An army was successfully used by Sulla to seize the dictatorship in 81 BC, and thereafter violence became endemic to Roman politics, becoming particularly serious in the 60s and 50s BC despite the passing of several laws *de vi* ('on force'). Violence was used to protest about shortages of corn and other popular grievances (especially in the 70s BC, when the restrictions imposed on the tribunes of the plebs reduced their potential for activity on behalf of the people); to disrupt assemblies, or to by-pass a veto imposed on a proposal by a tribune; or, more generally, to intimidate political opponents. A spiral of violence culminated in 52 BC with a pitched battle on the Appian Way near Bovillae (not far from Rome) between P. Clodius Pulcher and T. Annius Milo and their supporters, in which the former was killed. Clodius had been campaigning for the praetorship, and Milo (who had been energetic in supporting Cicero earlier in the 50s) for the consulship. Clodius' body was cremated by his supporters in the Senate House, which was completely destroyed in the process. Unprecedented measures were then taken to restore order, including the deployment of regular troops in the city itself. Three years later, Julius Caesar crossed the Rubicon with his army, entered Italy, and set in motion the civil war which was to bring about the end of the Republic.

A letter written by Cicero to his friend Atticus demonstrates the seriousness of the situation in the autumn of 57 BC, when Cicero had just returned from exile, and the extent to which acts of political violence had by then become an almost daily occurrence.

> 3 November: The builders were driven out from my site by armed men, and the portico of Catulus (which was being restored by decree of the senate and a consular contract, and had almost reached the level of the roof) was demolished. First of all they damaged the house of my brother Quintus by throwing stones at it from the site of my own house, then it was set alight on Clodius' orders, with firebrands thrown in view of the entire city...
>
> 11 November: While I was going down the Via Sacra, Clodius pursued me with his men. There was shouting, stones thrown, cudgels wielded, swords drawn: all of this quite unexpected. I withdrew into the vestibule of Tettius Damio; those who were

with me easily kept out the thugs.

12 November: Clodius tried to attack and burn Milo's house on the Cermalus, openly leading out – at eleven o'clock in the morning! – men armed with swords and shields, and others with burning firebrands. He had used the house of P. Sulla as a base for the assault. Q. Flaccus led out some strong men from Milo's other house: he killed some of the most notorious members of Clodius' gang.

19 November: Milo went to the Campus before midnight with a substantial force; Clodius, although he had his hand-picked squad of runaway slaves, did not dare to enter it himself.

(CICERO, *Letters to Atticus* 4.3)

Cicero's letter illustrates, too, the way in which violence had begun to mimic the supposedly peaceful processes of politics, which were tied to particular locations in the city. Aristocratic houses were traditionally scenes of political activity, with gatherings of clients and *amici* taking place in the *atrium*; now opponents' houses were being physically attacked, or used as places of refuge when violence broke out. In 75 BC, the consuls were attacked by a hungry mob while they were accompanying a candidate for the praetorship down the Via Sacra and pursued into the nearby house of Octavius. Even the ceremony of *salutatio* became dangerous, since the aristocrat's house was then open to all comers; it was alleged that the Catilinarian conspirators had plotted to assassinate Cicero while he was receiving visitors. Houses might be used as garrisons: when Milo's house came under attack following the murder of Clodius, we are told that Clodius' supporters were dispersed by a volley of arrows from within the house. The rioters, however, succeeded in breaking into the house of M. Aemilius Lepidus and smashing up the family portraits in his *atrium*. Similarly, Clodius' funeral was in some senses a parody of the traditional aristocratic funeral, with the body displayed in his *atrium*, escorted by a crowd down to the Forum, and orations made by his supporters from the Rostra, in a way that prefigured the similar treatment of the assassinated Julius Caesar. Occupation of the public spaces of the city by force became a standard way of taking control of political meetings. Cicero's letter to Atticus continues by describing Milo's strategy for disrupting the elections, which was to occupy the Campus Martius and watch for ill omens; if these were noted, it would mean that the elections would have to be postponed. Similarly, many violent incidents are described as taking place in the Comitium or in the Forum.

During the first century, levels of violence seem to have gone hand in hand with the increasing importance of *collegia* in the city. *Collegia* were popular associations which had a variety of different focal points: they might be associated with a particular trade, a particular neighbourhood of the city, or reverence for a particular shrine or deity. In practice, these categories often overlapped: those practising a particular profession often lived in the same part of the city and neighbourhoods were often identified by a notable local shrine. The exact nature of the activities of the republican *collegia* of the city of Rome is unclear, since they often operated on the limits of the legal; we know much more about the *collegia* of the imperial period, whose more 'respectable' activities were recorded on inscriptions. The *collegia* were, like any other religious or secular group standing apart from the formal political and patronage structures of the Roman state, regarded with extreme suspicion by the Roman authorities and were repeatedly banned. Legislation dissolving most of them was passed in 64 BC (perhaps in the context of the tensions leading up to the Catilinarian conspiracy), although they were legalised in 58 following new legislation introduced by Clodius, who then exploited the opportunities they offered; they were banned again by Julius Caesar, and – with some exceptions – by Augustus. In some ways the increasing importance of *collegia* can be linked to the possible decline of patronage in the city during the last decades of the Republic: immigrants to Rome were unlikely to have close links with a particular patron in the city, and membership of a *collegium* might be seen as an alternative. From what we know of the *collegia* in the imperial period, however, it is likely that they too were reliant collectively on patrons for financial and practical support. Cultivating the *collegia* and the *vici* (urban districts of the city) was a way of gaining support from the plebs, as the author of the *Commentariolum* saw; and just as members of the traditional aristocracy could employ clients in violent acts when necessary, so Clodius, who was particularly close to the leadership of many of the *collegia*, could draw on their support when violence was being planned.

Electoral strategies

A variety of possible electoral strategies was therefore available to the ambitious politician. These could also be combined in different permutations according to the background of a particular candidate and the type of support he sought. *Novi homines* (who seem to have been at a disadvantage, in the consular elections at least) would have to make special efforts, as the *Commentariolum* shows, to seek support from across Roman society; *nobiles* could rely more on their family's prestige. Although patronage had traditionally been, and continued to be, an important element in social relationships between the aristocracy and their social inferiors and could also be exploited to seek political support, there were other ways in which politicians could seek to influence the vote and these became increasingly important during the last hundred years of the Roman Republic. It was a long time since Rome had been the sort of small rural community in which the structures of patronage were most likely to flourish. Many who moved to Rome as the city expanded had no particular attachment to one individual patron or one particular family. Those 'close to the great houses', who were well placed to influence the upper centuries in the *comitia centuriata*, presumably had their own clients who might be equally influential in the lower centuries; but each might have divided loyalties in a fiercely contested election. Bribery could potentially be an effective way of gaining the support of some of the poorer citizens – though there was always the risk that the perpetrator might be prosecuted, in which case the election result might be set aside. As the strength of the ties of formal patronage between individuals weakened, and the population of Rome became more heterogeneous, especially in the first century BC, *collegia* became increasingly important; but since the state of their finances was often parlous and they often relied on the support of patrons themselves, they were not entirely divorced from the traditional structures of patronage. Sometimes, we might imagine, they paid their dues to their patron in the form of acts of violence.

Moreover, we should not forget that citizens also had the possibility of individual political choice, and politicians exploited this avenue in devising their campaigns, with efforts made to canvass individual voters. What exactly motivates a person to cast their vote for one candidate rather than another is not always clear in our own society, and still harder to discern in antiquity. The Romans, however, evidently felt that voters could be influenced by a man's reputation and achievements – whether as a military leader or an orator, the distinction of his family, influential support from well-known political figures, or a high profile resulting from an impressive house or unusual and memorable triumphal celebrations. Equally well, it is quite possible that a very substantial proportion of the electorate each year had little interest in the competing candidates or in the outcome of the vote and had no pressing reason to participate at all.

Late Republican politics: a sketch

Although the focus of the discussion in this book has primarily been on the political system at Rome, it would be a mistake to discuss politics independently of the broader economic, social and ideological context. This sketch will therefore attempt, if only briefly, to relate the changing nature of political activity in the last 150 years of the Republic to the broader historical context, as well as suggesting some possible ways through the controversies surrounding the political system of the later Republic. The main point to be stressed is the way in which changes in the system can be identified during the period of time under investigation – there were significant developments both in the formal constitutional arrangements at Rome and in the social and economic background: we ought therefore to look at debates about patronage, accessibility to the senate and popular participation with these trends in mind.

Aristocratic rivalry, which had long been a characteristic feature of life in Rome, became more competitive from the beginning of the second century BC onwards, with an intensity that no doubt reflected the influx of wealth resulting from Rome's successful (and lucrative) military campaigns in Greece and Asia Minor, and the economic opportunities offered by the growth of Rome's empire. Laws clamping down on bribery, luxury and repeated tenure of magistracies were introduced and reiterated. More junior magistracies were introduced to run the increasing numbers of overseas provinces, but this had the effect of aggravating the level of competition for the higher offices. However, in the latter half of the second century BC Rome became involved in a series of problematic wars in Spain, and the social tensions between rich and poor that had been concealed by the economic well-being resulting from imperial expansion began to re-emerge. Few if any colonies were established between 177 and 128 BC, so one traditional route to upward social mobility (though it involved losing political rights at Rome), that of joining a new community on the borders of Italy, had been closed off to the poor. Meanwhile, the increasing use of slave-based agriculture in some areas of the Italian countryside, in particular those such as coastal Etruria and northern Campania which were close to Rome and had ready access to the markets of the capital and the provinces, contributed further to the well-being of the upper classes. This was largely to the detriment of some sectors of the rural peasantry, as it often led to their being forced off the land. This type of agricultural exploitation was to become even more widespread in Italy in the first century BC. The tribunes of the plebs, after many years of apparent quiescence, began to take a newly radical role in political life, protesting about the burden of military service and the sufferings of the rural poor.

Probably late in the third century BC, the *comitia centuriata* had been reorganised to give additional weight to the votes of the lower voting units. In the latter part of the second century, the secret ballot was introduced to the assemblies and other initiatives implemented to reduce intimidation. All of these measures seem to have contributed, at least in a limited way, to democratising the assemblies – a trend reflected by the replacement of the Comitium by the (larger) Forum for meetings of the assembly. These initiatives gave greater influence to those of the citizens who attended the meetings. Yet the basic problem remained that regular attendance by those from outside Rome was very difficult except for the affluent and the highly motivated, and indeed became even more so with the grant of Roman citizenship to Rome's Italian allies after the Social War, and their eventual registration in the voting tribes in the years that followed. In the first century the *comitia centuriata* continued largely to be controlled by the wealthier classes, Italian as well as Roman. However, as the city of Rome grew and more and more Italians moved to the city (in part as a result of the economic and social pressures now being felt more widely across Italy), it seems likely that the *comitia tributa* came increasingly to involve those who had originated in the countryside but now lived in the city. Patronage decreased in importance, popular bodies like the *collegia* became more influential in the city, bribery became more extensive and acts of violence more frequent. By contrast, the rural poor beyond the periphery of Rome had on the whole little involvement with, or commitment to, the popular assemblies.

Although in reality the senate had predominant influence and authority in the state, the close relationship of Comitium and Curia, reflected in the Latin colonies newly created by Rome, symbolised the involvement of the People in government as well as the senate. An appeal to the decision of the People – deciding between rival candidates at election time – provided a way of resolving rivalries within the senate, while at the same time maintaining the solidarity and coherence of that body. The essential unity of the Roman senate and People, and their involvement together in political decision-making, was, perhaps surprisingly, a central element in the ideology of the Roman elite, as even traditionalist senators saw *concordia* between the different classes as an ideal to which the Roman state should aspire. Citizens, however grand or humble, had a collective identity that differentiated them from slaves or foreigners. Although the Roman people did potentially have a significant role to play at election time, yet the numbers of individuals actually involved – voting or participating in public meetings – were rather limited, and they formed a restricted and unrepresentative group within the citizenry as a whole. The competitive activities of the aristocracy beyond formal politics were similarly played out before select elements of the Roman people. Just as those participating in aristocratic funerals and watching the *ludi* put on by the elite tended in practice to be those closest to their patrons, and by implication the most affluent among the plebs, so those whose goodwill and electoral support was most valued were the comparatively wealthy.

The rural poor were almost entirely marginalised from these political relationships, however, and this was to lead to difficulties. The Italian elites were in the first century significantly involved in political activity at Rome, either mobilised by the traditional noble families or supporting the aspiring *novi homines*. For reasons of security, it was also essential for the political class at Rome in the late Republic to conciliate the urban masses, just as the emperors were to do in later years. The rural peasantry, which supplied either all or a great proportion of Rome's military man-power, was also of crucial importance to the Roman state. Moreover, the separation of military and political responsibility, which became most apparent in the first century BC (after Marius began to recruit soldiers from the landless poor, a trend further encouraged by the upheavals of the Social War), had potentially very serious implications. Not only were Rome's soldiers no longer involved in the political process; their leaders, too, tended in the years after Sulla's dictatorship to take up military or provincial commands late in their magistracy and in the following year, rather than campaigning extensively as praetor or consul, as had been the normal pattern in the second century. Their military and political identity became separated. Long years of military campaigning by the rural poor under the leadership of men like Pompey or Caesar, combined with the ambitious individualism of their commanders, were in the end to lead to civil war and the collapse of the Republic.

Chapter 6
The Empire: the end of politics?

The advent of the Empire, and of a single ruler, transformed the political scene at Rome. Since the death of Clodius and the destruction of the Senate House in 52 BC, the city had been in a state of almost continual political ferment. Troops had been deployed in the city to restore order, and three years later Julius Caesar led his army across the Rubicon into Italy, seizing power as his rival Pompey departed for Greece. Victorious in a series of battles around the Mediterranean, Caesar consolidated his power, repeatedly holding the offices of consul and *dictator*, and eventually taking on the role of *dictator* in perpetuity. On 15 March 44 BC, the Ides of March, he was assassinated by a group of conspirators which included Brutus and Cassius. Caesar's adoptive heir Octavian, M. Antonius (Mark Antony) and M. Aemilius Lepidus took control at Rome, established themselves in a triple magistracy as 'triumvirs' (*triumviri rei publicae constituendae*) and defeated Brutus and Cassius at the battle of Philippi in 42 BC. Their rule was characterised by violence – up to three hundred senators may have died in the 'proscriptions', officially sanctioned murders of the triumvirs' enemies, together with many equestrians – and by a chaotic abandonment of the traditional rules of politics at Rome, as the triumvirs themselves made appointments to magistracies (though the electoral machinery of the assemblies continued to function). In 39 BC consuls were appointed for eight years in advance; the following year, 67 praetors were appointed and a boy was made quaestor without even having taken on the toga of manhood. After Caesar's death the senate grew to contain more than a thousand members, including what Suetonius terms 'a shameful and uncouth crowd' (*Augustus* 35). Octavian's defeat of Antonius and his ally, the Egyptian queen Cleopatra, at the battle of Actium in 31 BC, left him as undisputed ruler of the Roman world. Two years later he celebrated a grand triumph and in 27 BC, taking on the new name of Augustus, set about the process which was known as the 'restoration of the Republic'.

Augustus' delicate task was to restore calm, confidence and political structures that were identifiable with the traditions of the Republic, without in the process actually losing his own pre-eminence in the state.

71

Suetonius describes how he 'restored the traditional authority of the *comitia*' (*Augustus* 40) and expelled large numbers from the senate, but it was less easy to break the cycle of bribery and violence which had characterised the late Republic. Serious disturbances occurred during a food shortage in 22 BC, when a mob blockaded the senators in the Curia and threatened to set the building on fire, and in 19 BC when murders and violence disrupted the consular elections. Even as late as AD 7 there was more violence and so Augustus personally appointed the magistrates. A *Lex Iulia de ambitu* was passed in 18 BC, clamping down on bribery, and Suetonius records that Augustus was accustomed to distribute funds to the members of the two voting tribes with which he was associated, the Fabia (that of the Julii, his adoptive family) and the Scaptia (that of the Octavii, his natural family), in order to discourage them from accepting bribes from others.

The basic structure of the popular assemblies was restored in line with republican practice, but some significant changes began to be introduced in the latter years of Augustus' life. In AD 5, the *Lex Valeria Cornelia* (known largely from an inscription discovered at the Etruscan town of Heba, and another subsequently found at Siarum in Spain) provided for the creation of ten special centuries in the *comitia centuriata*, consisting of senators and senior *equites*, which were named after Gaius and Lucius Caesar, Augustus' adoptive sons who had died young. Subsequently five more each were created in honour of Germanicus, adoptive son of the emperor Tiberius, who died in AD 19, and of Drusus, the natural son of Tiberius, who died in AD 23. These centuries took on the role formerly taken by the *centuria praerogativa*, by declaring their vote first and giving a lead to the assembly. The aim of the measure may have been to honour the senators and *equites*, or perhaps in order to discourage disorder at election-time by providing a clear lead from the wealthiest classes. The practical impact may well have been negligible, but one of the ostensibly 'republican' features of the *comitia centuriata* had been eroded.

According to Dio, although the popular assemblies continued to meet under Augustus, 'nothing was done which was not acceptable to him' (DIO 53.21). Augustus' exceptional standing in the state meant that an expression of support for a candidate resulted in his being elected, and for the greater part of his reign he made a point of canvassing in the traditional republican way. After AD 7, however, there was a subtle change in procedure: Augustus no longer attended the elections in person, but instead posted a list of approved candidates for all to see. In AD 14, just after Augustus' death, the election of magistrates was transferred to the senate, which 'was happy, having been freed from the necessity to engage in

sordid canvassing and distributions of money' (TACITUS, *Annals* 1.15).
Those who sought magistracies spoke in support of their own candidature, and other senators in support of those they favoured; an open vote then took place, members of the senate moving to one side of the Curia or the other to indicate their decision. The popular assemblies continued to meet, however, formally ratifying a list of candidates proposed to them by the senate, at least until the 3rd century AD. Caligula is said to have attempted to restore direct control over the elections to the assemblies, but was frustrated as in the event no more candidates presented themselves than there were places available, and he subsequently returned the elections to the senate.

The fact that the elections had been transferred to the senate, and that the emperor now produced a list of his recommended candidates, did not, perhaps surprisingly, bring about the end of electoral competition: there are numerous references in literature to hotly contested elections. In AD 60 there was such fierce competition in the elections for the praetorship that Nero created three additional praetorships, especially to allocate to the disappointed candidates. The Younger Pliny provides some graphic illustrations of the political rivalries of the late first and early second centuries AD: for instance early in the second century AD there was uproar in the senate as the secret ballot was introduced (just as its introduction in the popular assembly had been strongly opposed in the second century BC); the senate decreed that 'candidates should be prohibited from providing dinners, distributing gifts, and depositing money with agents' (*Letters* 6.19). Trajan similarly had to intervene to clamp down on excessive expenditure on the part of candidates. Lively competition continued to take place, but now within the setting of the senate. At least from the time of Tiberius, it was standard practice for the emperors to provide a list of their candidates – in fact, the *Lex de imperio Vespasiani*, a grant of powers to the emperor Vespasian on his accession to the principate in AD 69, enacted that candidates recommended by the emperor should be given special treatment in the elections. Although the consulships were now in practice allocated by the emperors, not all of the lower magistracies competed for were earmarked for the emperor's nominees. It became customary for those thinking of standing for office to approach the emperor for his permission. He could react in one of three ways: putting the candidate on the list of his recommended candidates, as a *candidatus Caesaris*; allowing him to stand (but without special support); or forbidding him to stand. This enabled competition to take place between those who had permission to present themselves but were not the designated candidates of the emperor, which explains why there continued to be lively political rivalry for the lower magistracies even after the advent of the imperial system.

The popular assemblies thus survived the advent of the empire, though for all practical purposes elections were now contested in the senate. There was now less risk of a breakdown of public order, since the military presence of the praetorian guard and the urban cohorts allowed the emperors to suppress disturbances more effectively than had been possible under the Republic. Bribery was not unknown, and patronage – of the emperor, and other distinguished figures in the senate – also had a substantial part to play in determining the outcome of the elections.

Cicero observed that:

> the judgement and will of the Roman people in matters of the public interest can be indicated most clearly in three settings: at a public meeting, at a voting assembly, and in the audience assembled for shows or gladiatorial combats.
>
> (CICERO, *In support of Sestius* 106).

Under the Empire, the popular assemblies declined in importance. Formal political *contiones* became much less frequent, although the emperor would on occasion address the people. Suetonius reports that Nero, about to be overthrown, had it in mind to make a speech to the people and throw himself on their mercy, but thought better of this scheme and the text of the speech was discovered in his desk after his death (SUETONIUS, *Nero* 47). A sculptured relief of the early second century AD depicts an emperor, probably Trajan or Hadrian, addressing the people in the Forum from the Rostra. *Ludi*, gladiatorial shows, and gatherings in the circus therefore became the main occasion on which the people could express their collective view, and these meetings were supported and encouraged by emperors. As Fronto (the orator and close associate of the Emperor Marcus Aurelius) observed, writing in the mid-second century AD:

> the emperor did not neglect actors or the other performers on the stage, the circus or the arena, knowing that the Roman people is held firm by two things above all, the corn supply and the shows. (FRONTO, *Introduction to history* 17).

The games provided an occasion at which emperor and people could meet, the emperor displaying his generosity to his citizens and enjoying the people's pleasures; but the people might also seize the opportunity to express their disapproval of his activities. Protests in the theatre led to

Tiberius returning a statue which he had removed to his palace from the Baths of Agrippa, and during the same emperor's reign there were also popular complaints about the high price of corn. Caligula, however, was less tolerant of such opposition and was said to have wished that the Roman people 'had only one neck' (SUETONIUS, *Caligula* 30); on one occasion, spectators at the games protesting at high levels of taxation were executed. At the theatre and at the games, the seating arrangements became increasingly organised according to rank during the late Republic and the early Empire, with special places allocated to different classes and groups within society; increasingly the collective identity of Roman society was expressed more in the circus or arena than in the formal political institutions of the state. The power over life and death held by the Roman people was represented not by trials in the *comitia centuriata*, but by the ability to condemn or liberate a defeated gladiator; executions now often took place in the arena, rather than at the *carcer* or the Tarpeian rock overlooking the Comitium and Forum.

The relationship between senate and emperor was a complex and difficult one. In some ways the prestige and importance of the senate had increased at the expense of that of the popular assemblies: after Augustus, elections now took place in the senate. Decrees of the senate, *senatus consulta*, increasingly came to replace *leges* passed by the assembly, though the emperor too played a role in legislation. The senate took on new judicial functions at the expense of the assemblies and those *equites* enrolled in panels to decide legal cases. Formally, the senate continued to maintain authority and both Augustus and Tiberius (in the earlier part of his reign) made a point of consulting it regularly. In reality, however, the advent of the emperor inevitably had the effect of limiting the power and prestige of both the senate and its individual members. Notionally, the empire was divided into the more peaceful public provinces, and the imperial provinces, which tended to be those where substantial military forces were stationed. Yet in practice the emperor clearly had control of the whole structure of the empire and was able to issue edicts which were obeyed in both types of province. Although both senate and emperor were involved in legislative activity, financial affairs and foreign policy increasingly became the sole concern of the emperor; it was usually he who received foreign delegations or initiated military campaigns. These restrictions on the senate collectively were paralleled by measures which restrained the competitive instincts of the individual senators. The last person outside the imperial family to celebrate a triumph was L. Cornelius Balbus, who had defeated the Garamantes in Africa in 19 BC. He constructed a theatre and portico, the *Theatrum* and *Crypta Balbi*, in the

Campus Martius between the Circus Flaminius and the Saepta: these were the last 'private' triumphal monuments to be built in Rome. From then on public building also became an activity restricted to the emperor and his family. In other ways too, competition with the emperor was discouraged: Augustus entrusted the task of organising gladiatorial games to the praetors and imposed a limit of 60 pairs of gladiators at each event, although he himself exhibited a total of 10,000 gladiators on just eight occasions.

The changing relationship of senate and emperor was marked by the changing locations in which the senate held its meetings. Augustus had completed the new Curia building initiated by Julius Caesar, but in the latter years of Augustus' reign the senate often met in the Temple of Apollo on the Palatine, adjacent to the palace. Although it was quite normal for the senate to meet in a temple, and there were practical reasons for holding the meetings there (especially following Augustus' serious illness in 23 BC, and when he became increasingly infirm with age) the symbolism of the senators climbing the hill to meet with the emperor (rather than the emperor descending the hill to meet with the senate) must have made the changing relationship between the senate and the emperor increasingly clear. Similarly, the 'commendation' of candidates by the emperor ultimately made him largely responsible not only for the appointment of consuls and other magistrates, but also (indirectly) for recruitment into the senate.

The Forum too was transformed by the activities of both Caesar and Augustus, though the latter was notably cautious in activities here (Fig. 9). The new Fora of Caesar and of Augustus allowed them to build on a more grandiose scale free of the constraints of the ancient buildings, sanctified by religion and tradition, which surrounded the Forum Romanum. The Curia was redesigned and constructed on a new alignment, now on a level with the Forum Romanum rather than significantly raised above it, and attached to the side of Caesar's Forum. A new Rostra was established by Caesar on the central axis of the Forum and this was provided with a new façade by Augustus, who may well have wished to eliminate the memory of the heads of the proscribed which had been displayed there under the triumvirate. At the opposite, eastern, end the Temple of the Divine Julius Caesar became a new focal point, with its own Rostra in front of it, and the Arch of Augustus, celebrating Augustus' diplomatic successes over the Parthians, beside it. The Portico of Gaius and Lucius Caesar was constructed in front of the basilica which lay along the north side of the Forum. Under Augustus the role of the Forum as a space for gladiatorial combats finally came to an end, as the underground passages were blocked up. The 'Golden Milestone' was set up near the Rostra, which served as a symbolic centre both of the city and of the Roman Empire as a whole.

In the Campus Martius, a permanent version of the Saepta constructed entirely in marble replaced the temporary enclosures of the republican period; this had been projected by Julius Caesar as early as 54 BC but was

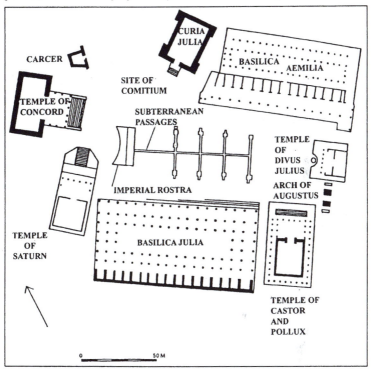

Fig 9 The Forum Romanum in the time of Augustus.

eventually completed in 26 BC by Agrippa. Soon after, with the decline of the *comitia*, it became a public space used largely for the holding of markets and gladiatorial games, or the display of works of art. The emperors followed the lead given by Pompey (who had constructed Rome's first permanent theatre there in 55 BC) and Statilius Taurus (an associate of Octavian who had given the city its first permanent amphitheatre in 29 BC), and built a whole series of monuments associated with entertainment and spectacle. These included the Baths of Agrippa and Nero, the Theatre of Marcellus, the Amphitheatre of Caligula, the Stadium of Domitian, together with more traditional temples and porticoes, and major imperial buildings such as Augustus' Mausoleum and Sundial. Far from being a place of formal political interaction and triumphal edifices, commemorating the achievements of the elite, the Campus was in the imperial period increasingly characterised by monuments for popular entertainment, and the display of imperial generosity to the plebs (see Fig. 5, p. 33). The *stabula factionum*, the headquarters of the teams of charioteers who performed in the circus, were now a more important feature of the Campus Martius than those of the *divisores*.

As the senate and the popular assemblies declined in importance, and as the emperors occupied more and more of the Palatine Hill with their palace, Roman aristocrats began to move away from the traditional centre of aristocratic housing on the slopes leading up from the Forum – a process that was further hastened by the destruction of much of the Palatine in the great fire of AD 64 under Nero and his confiscation of large swathes of the surrounding area to build his sumptuous new palace, the Golden House. Some aristocrats had always lived in parts of the city other than the Palatine, their houses surrounded by the homes of their clients and freedmen, but there are indications that under the empire the Aventine, the Esquiline, the Lateran, and the Caelian hills were increasingly favoured locations for the wealthy; some senators preferred to live outside Rome altogether, in grand villas on roads such as the Via Appia and Via Latina in the suburbs of the city. Where once the wealthiest Romans sought to live in close proximity to the Forum, the centre of their public life, increasingly the senators of the imperial period wanted to live on the periphery of the city. Given the unpredictable and jealous behaviour of some emperors there were attractions in living as far as possible out of view. The design of wealthy houses seems slowly to have changed from Republic to Empire: the *atrium* was no longer the main focus of the residence, yet the importance of peristyles and rooms for entertainment in the imperial house suggests that patronage continued to be an important element in the aristocratic lifestyle, but was predominantly a social rather than a political phenomenon. Aristocratic tombs, like the monument of Caecilia Metella on the Appian Way, had been becoming increasingly grandiose in scale up to the time of Augustus, but thereafter – since there was no longer scope to compete with structures like Augustus' Mausoleum on the Campus Martius – the elite chose instead to have themselves commemorated with modest and understated monuments, leaving the more ostentatious styles to upwardly mobile freedmen. Aristocratic competition was now largely a private, rather than a public phenomenon. It was the emperor who now sought the support and admiration of the People at triumphs, in the arena, and in the streets of Rome.

Suggestions for Further Study

1. How much (or how little) evidence has the historian to go on in reconstructing the topography of the city of Rome? Choose a monument and check up on the data available using, e.g. Richardson's *Topographical Dictionary of Ancient Rome*.

2. How democratic was the political system of the Roman Republic? You might like to compare it with (a) the classical Athenian democracy and (b) the political system of the country in which you live. Did the situation change significantly in the last 150 years of the Republic?

3. To what extent did the public buildings of the city of Rome reflect the changes in the political system at Rome in the late Republic? Choose an area of the city (e.g. Forum, Palatine, Campus Martius) and investigate how its appearance changed over the period.

4. How far did tombs and houses have political functions at Rome? Compare Roman practices with those in another society or culture with which you are familiar and think about possible explanations for the differences.

5. Imagine you are advising a candidate for office at Rome. Devise a strategy to maximise his chances of success in the elections. What difference would it make if the election is taking place in (a) the *comitia centuriata*, (b) the *comitia tributa*? In what ways would a campaign for a noble (*nobilis*) differ from that of a 'new man' (*novus homo*)?

6. In what ways did the advent of imperial rule affect the political system at Rome? Think about the functions of the senate, magistrates and popular assemblies under the Republic and how these changed under the Empire. What were the gains and losses for each of these groups?

Suggestions For Further Reading

There is a vast range of publications on the last century-and-a-half of the Roman Republic. The scale of the material available is illustrated by the fact that, in 1971, N. Criniti was able to identify 809 scholarly articles and books on the subject of the Catilinarian conspiracy in 63 BC alone (not to mention 14 novels, 70 plays, 4 operas and a film) – and many more have appeared since then. In this (very selective) bibliography I have deliberately concentrated on work published in English, though the wealth of important publications in other languages should of course not be forgotten. This is particularly true of studies on the topography of Rome, where the work of archaeologists such as A. Carandini (who directed excavation of the house of M. Aemilius Scaurus) F. Coarelli (who has published fundamental studies of the Forum Romanum, Forum Boarium and Campus Martius) and others has contributed very significantly to our understanding of the ancient city.

General and introductory reading

For accessible (and analytical) introductions to the history of the later Roman Republic and the structures of Roman politics, see P.A. Brunt, *Social Conflicts in the Roman Republic* (Chatto & Windus, 1971), and the introductory chapter in his *The Fall of the Roman Republic and Other Essays* (Oxford University Press, 1988); T.P. Wiseman (ed.) *Roman Political life 90 BC-AD 69* (University of Exeter Press, 1985); M. Beard & M.H. Crawford, *Rome in the Late Republic* (Duckworth, 1985; 2nd edn, forthcoming), and M.H. Crawford, *The Roman Republic* (Fontana, 2nd edn, 1992). For a more traditional narrative account, see H.H. Scullard, *A History of the Roman World 753-146 BC* (Methuen, 4th edn, 1980) and his *From the Gracchi to Nero* (Methuen, 5th edn, 1982); volumes 8 (1989) and 9 (1994) of the second edition of the *Cambridge Ancient History* (Cambridge University Press) provide both narrative and analysis.

Topography of Rome

The bibliography on the topography of Rome is vast, much of it published in Italian. The key work of reference is now M. Steinby (ed.) *Lexicon Topographicum Urbis Romae* (Quasar, 1993-). At the time of writing four volumes have been published, covering monuments with names beginning with the letters A-S, and the remaining volume is at an advanced stage of preparation. Most of the articles are in Italian but some of those on key sites discussed in this book are in English: e.g. T.P. Wiseman on 'Campus Martius', and N. Purcell on 'Forum Romanum'. L. Richardson's single-volume *Topographical Dictionary of Ancient Rome* (Johns Hopkins University Press, 1992) is smaller in scale, but entirely in English. Both these volumes contain useful collections of maps and plans, and E. Nash, *Pictorial Dictionary of Ancient Rome* (Zwemmer, 1961-62) provides good photographs of many monuments. There is an excellent and up-to-date guidebook to the monuments of ancient Rome by A. Claridge, *Rome: an Oxford Archaeological Guide* (Oxford University Press, 1998) which also provides a good introduction to the practicalities (and difficulties) involved in the topographical study of the city; for an account of the rediscovery of ancient Rome, see C. Moatti, *The Search for Ancient Rome* (Thames and Hudson, 1989). Recent(ish) publications on Rome are reviewed in J.R. Patterson, 'The city of Rome: from republic to empire', *Journal of Roman Studies* 82 (1992) pp. 186-215. J. Coulston & H. Dodge, *Ancient Rome: the Archaeology of the Eternal City* (forthcoming) will contain a series of articles on different aspects of the archaeology, history and topography of the city of Rome.

Chapter 3: The Roman political system in outline

The republican constitutional system is clearly outlined in H.F. Jolowicz & B. Nicholas, *Historical Introduction to the Study of Roman Law* (Cambridge University Press, 3rd edn, 1972) pp. 8-57; M.H. Crawford, *The Roman Republic* (Fontana, 2nd edn, 1992) helpfully tabulates the varying responsibilities of the different popular assemblies in Appendix 1. See now A. Lintott's *The Constitution of the Roman Republic* (Oxford University Press, 1999).

The popular assemblies

For the working of the assemblies, see L.R. Taylor, *Roman Voting Assemblies from the Hannibalic War to the Dictatorship of Caesar*

(University of Michigan Press, 1966); E.S. Staveley, *Greek & Roman Voting and Elections* (Thames and Hudson, 1972); C. Nicolet, *The World of the Citizen in Republican Rome* (Batsford, 1980); R. MacMullen, 'How many people voted?' *Athenaeum* 58 (1980) pp. 454-7; U. Hall, 'Greeks and Romans and the secret ballot', in E.M. Craik (ed.) *'Owls to Athens': Essays on Classical Subjects Presented to Sir Kenneth Dover* (Oxford University Press, 1990) pp. 191-9; A. Yakobson, 'Secret ballot and its effects in the late Roman Republic', *Hermes* 123 (1995) pp. 426-442.

Popular participation

For the current debates on the nature of popular participation in Roman politics, see in particular the work of F.G.B. Millar, who stresses the importance of the popular assemblies within the Roman system, and the ultimate dependency of the aristocracy on the popular vote: 'The political character of the Classical Roman Republic', *Journal of Roman Studies* 74 (1984) pp. 1-19; 'Politics, persuasion and the people before the Social War', *Journal of Roman Studies* 76 (1986) pp. 1-11; *The Crowd in Rome in the Late Republic* (University of Michigan Press, 1998). By contrast, there is a greater emphasis on the limits of participation in M.I. Finley, *Politics in the Ancient World* (Cambridge University Press, 1983) pp. 70-96; see also L.A. Burckhardt, 'The political elite of the Roman Republic: comments on recent discussion of the concepts *nobilitas* and *homo novus*', *Historia* 39 (1990) pp. 77-99; T.J. Cornell, *The Beginnings of Rome* (Routledge, 1995) pp. 377-80; and H. Mouritsen, *Plebs and Politics in the late Roman Republic* (forthcoming). For another view, stressing the nature of politics as spectacle, and the importance of popular affirmation of the elite, see A.J.E. Bell, 'Cicero and the spectacle of power', *Journal of Roman Studies* 87 (1997) pp. 1-22.

The senate and the problem of senatorial openness

For the problem of the openness of the senate, and the prevalence of the *nobiles* as consuls, see K. Hopkins, *Death & Renewal* (Cambridge University Press, 1983) pp. 31-119 and E. Badian, 'The consuls, 179-49 BC', *Chiron* 20 (1990) pp. 371-413; also, with a particular emphasis on the terminology of *novi homines* and *nobiles* (and its implications) P.A. Brunt, *'Nobilitas & novitas'*, *Journal of Roman Studies* 72 (1982) pp. 1-17; D.R. Shackleton Bailey, *'Nobiles & novi* reconsidered', *American Journal of Philology* 107 (1986) pp. 255-60.

For discussion of political space in the centre of the city see F.G.B. Millar, 'Political power in the mid-republic: *curia* or *comitium*?', *Journal of Roman Studies* 79 (1989) pp. 138-50, and N. Purcell, 'Forum Romanum' in *Lexicon Topographicum Urbis Romae* vol. 2 (1995) pp. 325-42. The locations where the senate met during the Republic are analysed by M. Bonnefond-Coudry in *Le sénat de la république romaine* (École française de Rome, 1989) pp. 25-197. The most recent study of the Comitium is by P. Carafa, *Il Comizio di Roma dalle origini all'età di Augusto* (L'Erma di Bretschneider, 1998).

J. North valuably ties together several themes in recent work on Roman republican politics, in his 'Democratic politics in Republican Rome', *Past & Present* 126 (1990) pp. 3-21.

Chapter 4: Aristocratic competition in the city of Rome

For the competitive ethos of the Roman elite, see T.P. Wiseman (ed.) *Roman Political life 90 BC-AD 69* (University of Exeter Press, 1985) pp. 3-19; W.V. Harris, *War & Imperialism in Republican Rome 327-70 BC* (Oxford University Press, 2nd impression with new introduction, 1984) pp. 10-41; K.J. Hölkeskamp, 'Conquest, competition and consensus: Roman expansion in Italy and the rise of the *nobilitas*', *Historia* 42 (1993) pp. 12-39; T. Wiedemann, *Cicero and the End of the Roman Republic* (Bristol Classical Press, 1994) pp. 1-6. H. Flower, *Ancestor Masks and Aristocratic Power in Roman Culture* (Oxford University Press, 1996) is relevant to many of the themes discussed here.

Competition, military glory, triumphs and public building

The triumph is discussed in H. Versnel, *Triumphus: An Inquiry into the Origin, Development and Meaning of the Roman Triumph* (Brill, 1970); K. Hopkins, *Conquerors & Slaves* (Cambridge University Press, 1978) pp. 25-7; H.H. Scullard, *Festivals and Ceremonies of the Roman Republic* (Thames and Hudson, 1981) pp. 213-18.

For the building of temples and other public monuments under the Republic, see J.E. Stambaugh, *The Ancient Roman City* (Johns Hopkins University Press, 1988) pp. 16-47; F. Coarelli, 'Public building in Rome between the Social War and Sulla', *Papers of the British School at Rome* 45 (1977) pp. 1-23; A. Ziolkowski, *The temples of mid-Republican Rome* (L'Erma di Bretschneider, 1992); E.M. Orlin, *Temples, Religion and Politics in the Roman Republic* (Brill, 1997).

Competition and the aristocratic house

For aristocratic housing see T.P. Wiseman, 'Conspicui postes tectaque digna deo' in *Historiography and imagination: eight essays on Roman culture* (University of Exeter Press, 1994) pp. 98-115; the discussion in A. Wallace-Hadrill, *Houses and Society at Pompeii and Herculaneum* (Princeton University Press, 1994) pp. 3-16 is also relevant to the situation at Rome. The house of Aemilius Scaurus is discussed in A. Carandini, *Schiavi in Italia* (La Nuova Italia Scientifica, 1988) pp. 359-87.

Aristocratic funerals and commemoration

For tombs and funerary rituals, see J.M.C. Toynbee, *Death and Burial in the Roman World* (Thames and Hudson, 1971); K. Hopkins, *Death and Renewal* (Cambridge University Press, 1983) pp. 201-56. Gladiatorial combat has been a particular focus of interest in recent years: see, for example, K. Hopkins, *Death and Renewal* (Cambridge University Press, 1983) pp. 1-30, T. Wiedemann, *Emperors and Gladiators* (Routledge, 1992) and (for the holding of games in the Forum) K. Welch, 'The Roman arena in late-republican Italy: a new interpretation', *Journal of Roman Archaeology* 7 (1994) pp. 59-80.

Luxury, sumptuary laws and repeated tenure of magistracies

Sumptuary laws are discussed by D. Daube, *Roman Law: Linguistic, Social and Philosophical Aspects* (Edinburgh University Press, 1969) pp. 117-28 and A.W. Lintott, 'Imperial expansion and moral decline in the Roman Republic', *Historia* 21 (1972) pp. 626-38. For laws restricting repeated tenure of magistracies, see R. Develin, *Patterns in Office-holding 366-49 BC* (Latomus, 1979) pp. 81-95.

Chapter 5: The practice of politics

A guide to electioneering

The *Commentariolum Petitionis* is translated by D.W. Taylor and J. Murrell as *A short guide to electioneering* = *LACTOR* 3 (2nd edn, 1994); a translation by M.I. Henderson is also available in the *Loeb Classical Library* series in Cicero, *Letters to his Friends* vol. 4 (1972) with a useful introduction. See also J.S. Richardson '*The commentariolum petitionis*', *Historia* 20 (1971) pp. 436-42, for discussion of the authenticity of the text, and (most recently) R. Morstein-Marx, 'Publicity, popularity and patronage in the *Commentariolum Petitionis*', *Classical Antiquity* 17

(1998) pp. 259-88. On the political strategies adopted by *novi homines* in the first century BC, see T.P. Wiseman, *New Men in the Roman Senate* (Oxford University Press, 1971) pp. 95-142, and H. Mouritsen, *Italian Unification* (Institute of Classical Studies, 1998) pp. 95-8.

Patronage

The importance (or otherwise) of patronage in politics is discussed by P.A. Brunt, *The Fall of the Roman Republic and Other Essays* (Oxford University Press, 1988) pp. 382-442 and A. Wallace-Hadrill 'Patronage in Roman society: from Republic to Empire' in A. Wallace-Hadrill (ed.) *Patronage in ancient society* (Routledge, 1989) pp. 63-88.

Bribery

On bribery see the papers by A.W. Lintott, 'Electoral bribery in the Roman Republic', *Journal of Roman Studies* 80 (1990) pp. 1-16; A. Yakobson, '*Petitio et largitio*: popular participation in the centuriate assembly of the Late Republic', *Journal of Roman Studies* 82 (1992) pp. 32-52.

Violence

On violence, see A. Lintott, *Violence in Republican Rome* (Oxford University Press, 2nd edn, 1999); E.S. Gruen, *The Last Generation of the Roman Republic* (University of California Press, 1974) pp. 405-47; P.J.J. Vanderbroeck, *Popular Leadership and Collective Behaviour in the Later Roman Republic* (Gieben, 1987); and W. Nippel, *Public Order in Ancient Rome* (Cambridge University Press, 1995).

Chapter 6: The Empire: the end of politics?

For general discussion of the Augustan principate, see A. Wallace-Hadrill, *Augustan Rome* (Bristol Classical Press, 1993) and the essays by J.A. Crook in *Cambridge Ancient History* vol. 10 (Cambridge University Press, 2nd edn, 1996); P. Zanker's *The Power of Images in the Age of Augustus* (University of Michigan Press, 1988) is fundamental. See also D. Favro, *The Urban Image of Augustan Rome* (Cambridge University Press, 1996).

For the senate and assemblies under the triumvirate and then the Empire, see F.G.B. Millar, 'Triumvirate and principate', *Journal of Roman Studies* 63 (1973) pp. 50-67; the article by B. Levick in T.P.

Wiseman (ed.) *Roman Political life 90 BC-AD 69* (1985) pp. 45-68; P.A. Brunt, 'The role of the Senate in the Augustan regime', *Classical Quarterly* 34 (1984) pp. 423-44; R.J.A. Talbert, 'Augustus & the Senate', *Greece & Rome* 31 (1984) pp. 55-62, and his *The Senate of Imperial Rome* (Princeton University Press, 1984).

W. Eck, 'Senatorial self-representation: developments in the Augustan period' in F.G.B. Millar & E. Segal (eds.), *Caesar Augustus: Seven Aspects* (Oxford University Press, 1984) pp. 129-67, discusses the limits on senatorial display brought about by the advent of the Empire.

Glossary

For the convenience of the reader, Latin terms used in the book are listed here, with references to the main text as appropriate. For more detail, see entries in S. Hornblower & A. Spawforth (eds), *The Oxford Classical Dictionary*, 3rd edition (Oxford University Press, 1996).

adsectatores those who accompany a candidate during his electoral campaign.

aedilis (aedile) magistrate with responsibility for the day-to-day running of Rome, the games, and the corn-supply. Curule aediles were elected by the *comitia tributa*, plebeian aediles by the *concilium plebis*.

ambitus bribery of the electorate: literally means 'going round' the voters.

amicus 'friend', though the term might be used to refer to a political associate as well as someone with a close personal attachment.

atrium large reception room close to the entrance of an aristocrat's house, where clients would be entertained.

augur priests with particular expertise in the taking of auspices. They were on hand at election meetings in case omens were observed which might affect the proceedings.

candidatus a candidate for election, so called after his shining white toga. Under the Empire, a *candidatus Caesaris* was one who had the recommendation of the emperor, and so was certain to be elected.

capite censi the poorest citizens at Rome 'counted by heads alone' who were registered in a single century in the *comitia centuriata*.

carcer a dungeon adjacent to the Forum used for the execution of condemned criminals.

censor senior magistrate responsible for reviewing the senate and taking the census of Roman citizens, elected by the *comitia centuriata*.

centuria praerogativa voting century selected by lot to vote first in the *comitia centuriata*.

clientela a Roman aristocrat's clients.

cognomen a Roman's third name (e.g. Cicero), which followed the *praenomen* (e.g. Marcus), and the *nomen* (e.g. Tullius).

collegium a popular association or club, associated with a trade, a district in the city, or devotion to a particular cult.

comitia centuriata hierarchically organised voting-assembly of 193 centuries which elected censors, consuls and praetors.

comitia curiata archaic assembly composed of 30 *curiae*.

comitia tributa voting assembly of 35 tribes which elected quaestors and curule aediles.

comitium enclosure for meetings of the popular assembly located between the Forum and Senate House.

concilium plebis assembly of the plebs, similar to the *comitia tributa* but with patricians excluded.

concordia the ideal of 'concord' or 'harmony'. The Temple in the Forum Romanum dedicated to Concord was the scene of the 'trial' of the Catilinarian conspirators in 63 BC.

consul one of the two chief magistrates of the state, elected by the *comitia centuriata*.

contio informal meeting of an assembly at which magistrates would address the Roman People.

curia the Senate House. The term is also used to refer to the voting units in the *comitia curiata*.

cursus honorum fixed sequence in which magistracies were to be held; minimum ages for each office were introduced by the *Lex Villia Annalis* (180 BC).

deductores clients who accompanied an aristocrat down to the Forum.

dictator single chief magistrate appointed in time of political or military crisis during the early and mid-Republic; the office was also held by Sulla and Julius Caesar.

divisores agents who distributed bribes to the voting tribes.

equites ('equestrians') wealthy individuals (owning more than 400,000 sesterces) who were not members of the senate.

lex law passed by an assembly of the Roman people.

ludi 'games' held at religious festivals which included dramatic performances '*ludi scaenici*' and chariot-racing.

nobilis variously defined as a man with a consul, magistrate or patrician among his ancestors.

novus homo a man without senatorial ancestors who nevertheless entered the senate.

optimates 'the best men', traditionalists within the Roman aristocracy who laid emphasis on the authority of the senate.

ovile 'sheepfold' colloquial name given to the voting enclosure (otherwise known as the Saepta) on the Campus Martius.

patricians (*patricii*) prestigious hereditary group within the Roman elite, dating back to the early Republic or the regal period. By the late Republic their numbers had declined and their privileges consisted primarily of the exclusive right to hold certain priesthoods.

plebeians (*plebs*) all Romans who were not patricians; or, alternatively, the mass population of the city of Rome.

pomerium the ritual boundary of the city of Rome.

praetor magistrate elected by the *comitia centuriata*, with judicial or military responsibilities; next in line to the consul in the *cursus honorum*.

proletarii the poorest citizens at Rome 'capable only of producing children for the state' who were registered in a single century in the *comitia centuriata*.

quaestor junior magistrate, often with financial responsibilities, elected by the *comitia tributa*.

saepta voting enclosure on the Campus Martius, otherwise known as *ovile* (sheepfold) or (in the Empire) as Saepta Iulia.

salutatio daily ceremony at which clients (*salutatores*) greeted their patron in the *atrium* of his house.

stoa Greek term for a colonnaded public building.

templum ritually defined space laid out by the *augurs*, often, but not always, a temple in the sense of a building dedicated to a deity.

tribunus plebis (tribune of the plebs) magistrate elected by the *concilium plebis* to protect the interest of the plebeians. They could summon the *concilium plebis* and veto laws or acts of magistrates.

Index